DISCOVERING

THE NEW FOREST

Discovering the New Forest

Patricia Sibley
&
Robin Fletcher

ROBERT HALE · LONDON

First published in Great Britain 1986

Robert Hale Limited
Clerkenwell House
Clerkenwell Green
London EC1R 0HT

British Library Cataloguing in Publication Data

Sibley, Patricia
Discovering the New Forest.
1. Natural history—England—New Forest
2. New Forest (England)—Description and travel—Guide-books
I. Title II. Fletcher, Robin
574.9422'75 QH138.N4

ISBN 0-7090-2583-1

Photoset in North Wales by
Derek Doyle & Associates, Mold, Clwyd.
Printed in Great Britain by
St Edmundsbury Press, Bury St Edmunds, Suffolk.
Bound by Hunter & Foulis Limited.

Contents

For our friend
Barbara Wakeford
of Lymington

List of Illustrations

Living in the New Forest: *Between pages 184 and 185*

All photographs taken by Robin Fletcher

Maps

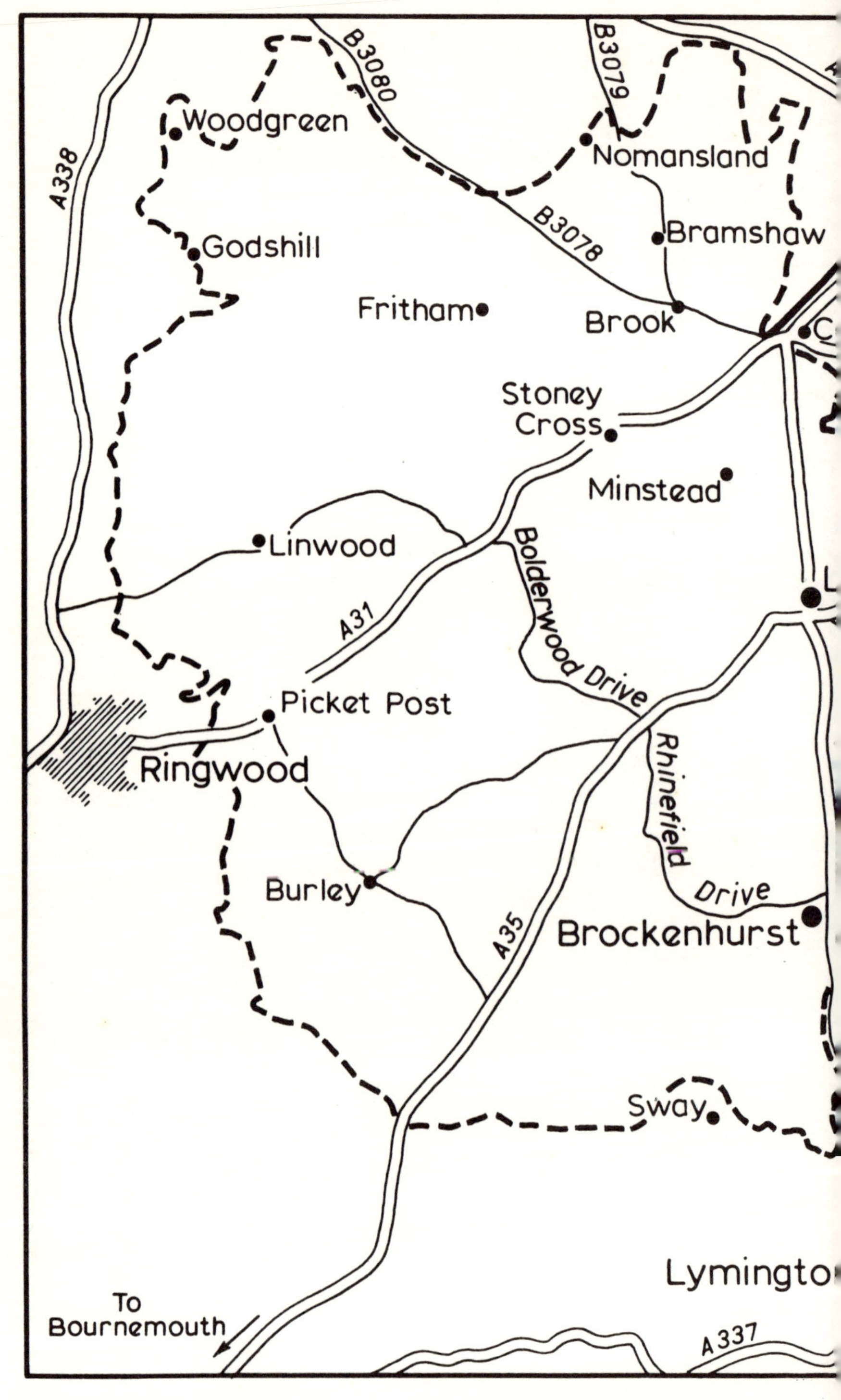

B3080
B3079
A338
Woodgreen
Nomansland
B3078
Bramshaw
Godshill
Fritham
Brook
Stoney
Cross
Minstead
Linwood
Bolderwood Drive
A31
Picket Post
Ringwood
Rhinefield
Drive
Burley
A35
Brockenhurst
Sway
Lymingto
To
Bournemouth
A337

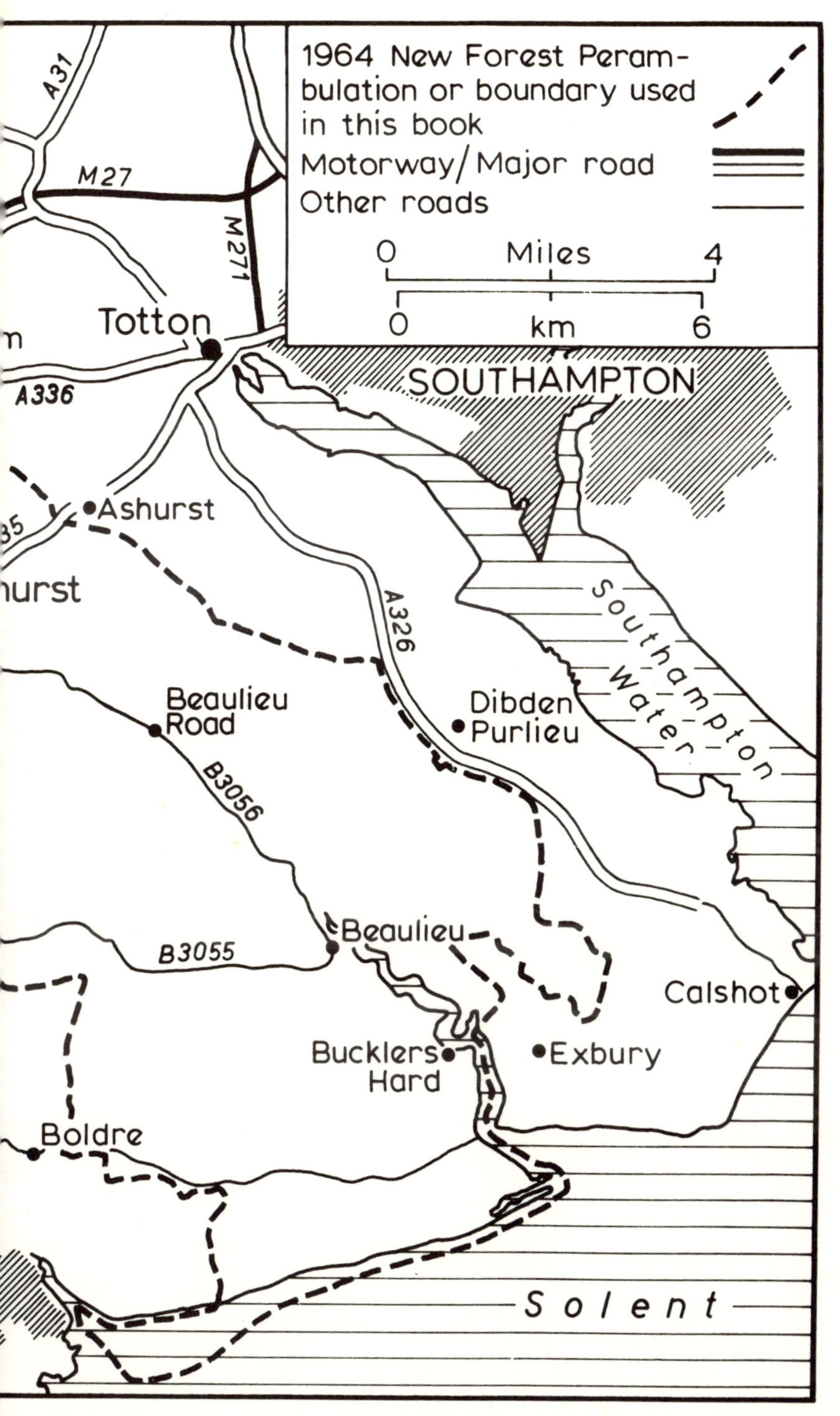
1964 New Forest Perambulation or boundary used in this book
Motorway/Major road
Other roads
0
Miles
4
0
km
6
A31
M27
M271
Totton
A336
SOUTHAMPTON
Ashurst
A326
Southampton Water
Dibden Purlieu
Beaulieu Road
B3056
Beaulieu
B3055
Calshot
Bucklers Hard
Exbury
Boldre
Solent

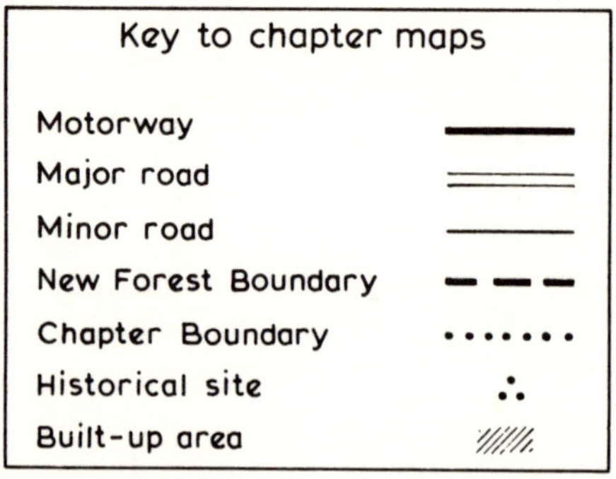

Key to chapter maps
Motorway
Major road
Minor road
New Forest Boundary
Chapter Boundary
Historical site
Built-up area

Acknowledgements

Our grateful thanks to all those who so readily gave us their time and help. We should like particularly to thank:

Jim Hooper of Woodgreen; Airlee Finn AI of Arniss Stables; R. Westlake of Sandy Balls; Hyde Band; Tony Russell of the Forestry Commission; Eric Ashby of Linwood; Roy Deacon of Linwood; Anne Rose of Rockford; Louise Martindale of Linwood; Sir Dudley Forwood, Bart.; Felicity Hardcastle of Burley; The Queen's Head, Burley; Burley Manor Hotel; Peter May of Holmsley; Miss Foster and Miss Douglas of Yaldhurst; Peter Chappell of Spinners Garden; Mrs Pike of Shirley Holms; Lesley Harnatt for the Beaulieu Estate; Kate Glegg of the Countryside Educational Trust; Terry Drew of Exbury Gardens; James Venner, Warden of North Solent National Nature Reserve; Mr Hardman of Rhinefield House; Harry Burt of South Weirs; Archie Cleveland, Verderer; Greta Hopkinson; New Forest Wagons; Mr Thomas of New Park; John Chalk, Huntsman, and Mrs Miller, Joint Master New Forest Buckhounds; Miss King of Foxlease; Joanna Osman, Angel's Farm Pottery; Mrs Cooper of Acres Down; Minstead Village Store; Dr McAll of Bignell Wood; Eileen of Minstead Lodge; D&B Renshaw of Little Skymers; Furzey Gardens, Minstead; Jack Ealing, Head Keeper, Forestry Commission; Jasper Corke of Langley Butterfly Farm; Bartley Pottery; Freda Harding, Burley Lodge; Mrs Pam Harvey Richards of the Green Dragon, Brooke; Reg King of Bramshaw; Mr and Mrs Thompson of Cuckoo Hill; Donald Cross for permission to use his book

Ringwood Industries; Roy Jackman for permission to use his compilation *Lyndhurst Past & Present*; David Stagg, Verderer, both for permission to quote from his book *New Forest Documents 1244-1334*, and for reading the manuscript; Anne Marks for typing the manuscript.

Preface

The New Forest has been well known and loved by us both for many years. To re-discover it, we divided the forest into eight areas, each with a town or village as its focal point, then travelled round each one, largely on foot, looking at buildings, talking to forest people, studying its industries and wild life, looking back at history and forward to to-morrow's problems, to present this unique country as it is today.

P.S.
R.F.

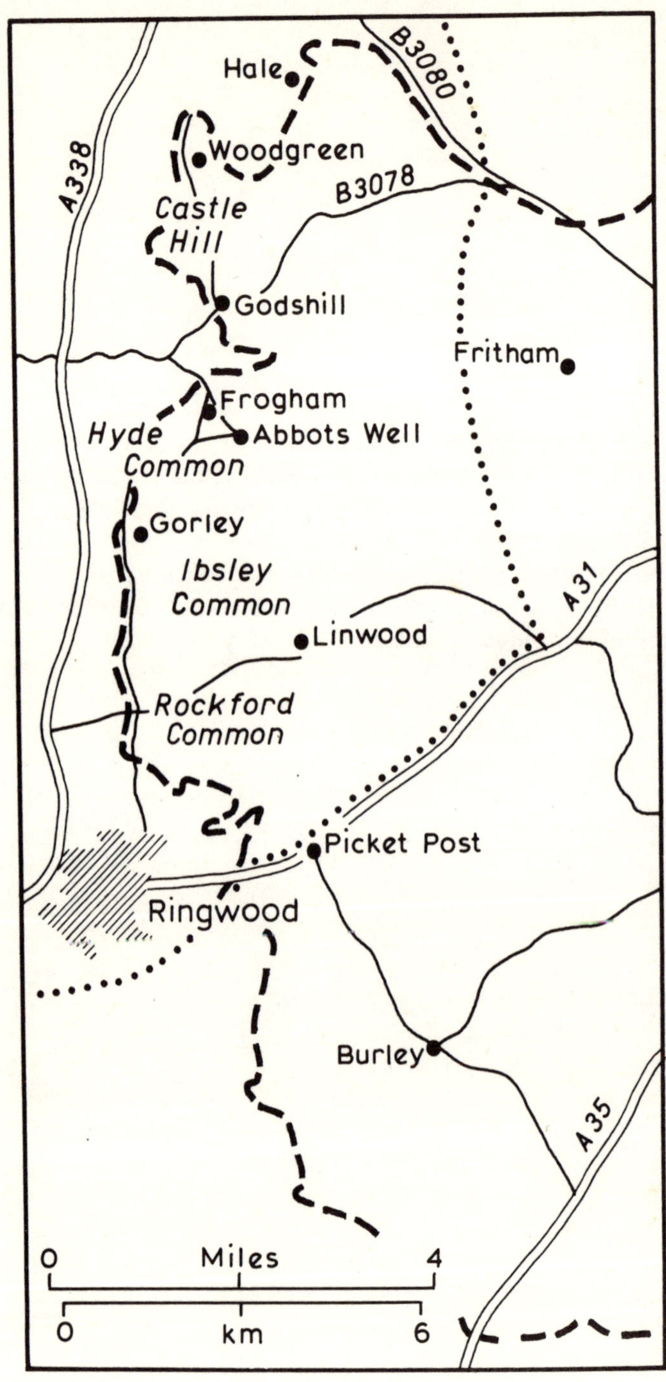

Ringwood and the Western Forest

1 *Ringwood and the Western Forest*

Winter-brown heathland slopes down from the ridge to green lawns by a stream, where chestnut ponies graze: beyond rise conifer woods, marching wind-tattered across the skyline, while to the south lie the ancient woods of oak and beech. Three fallow deer move away into the pines, white rumps conspicuous against dark trees, and a robin sings briefly from a solitary thorn; otherwise little moves on the chill air till the afternoon ride trots into sight on the white road over the ridge – yellow anoraks, red jackets, a girl calling out, 'I galloped, I galloped!'

Behind us lay the small pink cottage where Juliet de Bairacli Levy bathed in the dew, talked to the gypsies and wrote *Wanderers in the New Forest*, while a step down the lane leads to the waters of Abbots Well, fabled for its curative powers.

So here, high above Latchmore Bottom, meet all the threads which weave the pattern of this book, the lovely variety of New Forest countryside, its villages and hamlets, animals and birds, folklore and writers, together with the sweeping changes brought about by the Forestry Commission since 1972 (no cars may use that white road over Hampton Ridge) and the many ways of enjoying the forest.

This north-west land, of high parallel ridges between valley brooks running down to the Avon, is the least-known part, remote from 'honey pot' and ornamental drive; even roads are few. You can walk all day, as we shall later, through the woods of Sloden, Amberwood, Island Thorns, meeting only a Forestry worker brashing a plantation to remind you that the forest is a working place too.

To begin discovering the New Forest, still rich in secrets and deep-hidden places, we begin in the north-west corner at Hale, scattered among copses and fields. A wide green might seem the centre, with the village hall, a sunken way to the woods and some picturesque thatched cottages – the one with 'eyebrow' dormers used to be the dame school. A lane winds past the farm, and we might easily think that was Hale, but there is a clue on the left, a small squat stone building with incongruous Greek pillars along its front, a line of tall trees behind, Hatchet Lodge. Following the road we come to the ancient heart of Hale, the church and manor.

A road unfortunately now bisects the drive: originally it curved round from the Greek lodge between tall limes, said to be the longest avenue of its kind in England: even now the stretch from road to house is impressive. (Since this leads to the church car-park, there is a right of way.) Walk down it in April with the limes coming into first leaf, daffodils drifted over the grass beneath and ahead the stately pink walls of Hale House, with its Ionic portico.

Towards the end of the sixteenth century Elizabeth Paulet and her mother 'sold and squandered away all the patrimony of this ancient family', and so Hale came into the hands of the Penruddocks, but it is the Archers who have left their mark on the land. Thomas Archer, an architect, bought Hale Park in 1715. Groom Porter to Queen Anne, and subsequently George I and George II, he had control of gaming tables in the royal palaces which yielded annual 'perks' of £1,000, a huge sum at that time. This enabled him to travel, study Italian architecture at first hand and build Heythorpe Hall in Oxfordshire.

Later, at Hale, he pulled down the old house and designed the present one on classical lines as was the eighteenth-century fashion – hence the pillared lodge. Thomas Archer also designed St John's Church, Westminster, and the Cascade in Chatsworth grounds.

Following a track round to the right, we found a car-park, on a ledge, and down some steps, on a lower one, the church. Here we are on the very edge of the forest plateau where it falls in a steep escarpment to the river. Bowered in rhododendron and laurel on three sides, the churchyard commands a beautiful view of the Avon curving through its water-meadows below and away beyond over green Dorset distances.

The small, cruciform church is closely tied with the history of Hale House. Only the nave remains of the original church, still with its original stone benches along the walls, to remind us of the days when everyone stood in church and only 'the weakest went to the wall'.

The Penruddocks are remembered by a well-kept floor brass dated 1600. The church register for 1631 has this entry: 'This year the church walls were newly laid and raised, but the church roof was not laid till the next year following at the cost of Sir Thomas Penruddock, Bart.'

Thomas Archer added transepts, one wall being entirely taken up by the memorial he designed for himself, where he reclines in Roman dress on an elevated bath-shape high above the common herd. The north transept contains less florid memorials to the Goff family, owners of Hale in Victorian times, when a musicians' gallery stood above the west door. In 1895 a new roof was built, from timber grown on the estate.

The church still needs money for its maintenance and raises it in a unique way. One of the congregation gives sponsored rides – in his hot-air balloon! Since this transport was not available, we left Hale Church by a long flight of steps leading down to the lower road by the Avon, which brought us to Woodgreen.

Lying on a slope between high forest and river in this isolated corner, Woodgreen was once renowned as a wild place, inhabited by squatters and gypsies, where a stranger would get short shrift, since the gypsies sometimes murdered even each other in drunken brawls and the local witch could turn herself into a hare at will! Notorious for violence were the 'Merry Sundays' held in summer when the merries, or cherries, were ripe. Folk would flock into Woodgreen for the picking and the day degenerated from a fair to drunken squabbles and fights.

As late as the 1920s the locals were taking the law into their own hands. A woman accused the vicar of 'interfering' with Boy Scouts, but he was acquitted in court, so the villagers 'tin pannied' the woman for two nights, marching round her house till daylight banging pans, tins and fire irons, but on the third carrying her effigy round in a coffin which they subsequently burned up on the common. Even today, we were told, 'Tidn' a place where you doffs your cap.'

However, on a sunny February morning the village looked ordinary enough, red-brick Horse and Groom, the post office, village hall, small church and scatter of houses round a very small triangular green, just big enough to hold the bus shelter.

The church is bare, modern, white walls and light chairs, saved from austerity by pale blue carpet, deep blue west wall and a ceiling above the altar painted with the emblems of St Boniface. It was built in 1920. Next door, unpretentious, low-built, stands an ordinary-looking village hall, but inside one of the treasures of the forest, not to be missed.

In 1931 the Royal College of Art, with a grant from the Carnegie Trust, commissioned two of its students, R. Baker and E.R. Payne, to paint murals round the hall interior, and there they stand today only a shade faded, a complete and beautifully detailed picture of Woodgreen life more than fifty years ago, moreover containing portraits of everyone who lived in the village at that time.

The first panel shows a picturesque bend of the Avon from the forest edge, a heron flying over, a dog in the bracken and two countrymen tactfully painted with their backs to us – because of course they are poachers! For hundreds of years the illicit taking of game was a way of life, sometimes the only way a man could feed his family, comparable with smuggling along the coast. There are records as early as 1276 that John of Godshill, the neighbouring village, was accused of offences concerning vert and venison – that is, taking wood and deer, for which he was sent to prison and later fined. Poaching was not confined to the peasantry either: the Abbot of Beaulieu and the Bishop of Winchester, *en route* from the Isle of Wight, were also offenders.

Panel two, in total contrast, is a chapel anniversary picture, little girls and boys stiff in their best, looking impossibly good.

Next, the local girls in long dresses are dancing to a fiddle on the grass, while cherry trees in full bloom light the background – the famous merry trees which yielded big black juicy fruit with very small stones. The birds were a terrible problem as the fruit ripened, and many were shot. Bells were hung in the trees with long ropes attached, the other ends being taken through windows and secured to bed legs so that they could be rung in the early morning without too much effort. In the 1930s Woodgreen had a keen group of folk dancers who won the Hampshire championships; now there are not enough younger people to keep a team going. Here we heard the first complaint, to be repeated in many other places, that the village had an ageing population because there was nowhere for young married couples to live, property being snapped up for weekend cottages by 'foreigners' outside the Forest better able to pay inflated prices.

Panel four of the mural is a whole panorama of village goings-on, horses waiting patiently outside the Horse and Groom, a cow being milked, goats grazing on land which is now the cemetery, apple-picking, women gathering currants, bees and their hives. Honey was important not only for eating but as the chief ingredient of mead, a highly alcoholic drink. A great drinking place, Woodgreen: even the cattle were fed with hop mash fetched from Salisbury breweries.

Panel five is the annual flower show, decorous and pretty but with panel six we are back with the drink – orchards and cider-making. The cricket match used to have an annual home fixture with a team from Royal Navy ships in Portsmouth Harbour. The locals always elected to bat first – that is, before the lunch break of sandwiches and cider, and always won the match thanks to their secret weapon, a tot of mead lacing each visitor's drink! The visiting team seemed to go to pieces when they went in to bat …

The last full-size panel is a scene in Salisbury infirmary, but from the gable end above the stage the artists themselves look down at us from a hayfield.

The murals were very gently washed down some fifteen years ago. For a time the hall was open for viewing on Sunday afternoons. Now it is kept locked but the key can be obtained from a cottage opposite. You can also see a file of drawings and sketches from which the pictures were scaled up.

Just along the road lies the largest complex of glasshouses we had ever seen. Until recently this was a vast nursery called 'The

House of Flowers' and open to the public. Now it has been taken over by a company called Plant Technology, who are specialists in researching techniques for improving the production of food crops.

Turning up the lane we came to a vast green, unspoiled and lovely, the narrow road half encircling it past thatched cottages on one side, grazing cattle and ponies on the other, though fenced off the famous cricket pitch. A stranger might easily take this for the green of Woodgreen, but no, it is called the Common.

A lane brought us back to the forest edge. Behind lay Godshill Wood, Corsican pine and Norway spruce dark against the winter sky, a flock of great tits on its edge the only flash of colour. But in front of us stretched Dorset once again. All round lay the grassy pits and mounds, banks and ditches of an ancient castle, half overgrown with holly and oak. Castle Hill is the remains of an ancient stronghold splendidly positioned, for its western edge falls in places almost sheer down to river level, where the Avon, here wandering in great meanders, made one more line of defence.

Even on a cold day the viewpoint car-park is a good place for a picnic. Near at hand we watched tree creepers working mouselike up the bark of an oak, while far below three swans were sailing up to Breamore Mill.

Godshill village straggles along narrow lanes, a mix of old and new houses, across a ford, up a hill to the pub, the Fighting Cocks. Opposite on a wide expanse of green common we could still find the pit where this cruel sport was carried on, bets laid on the most promising birds: now only a lark sprang up from the nearest gorsebush and three rooks flew over toward Pitts Wood.

East and south-east of us the Forest stretches for miles without a metalled road, Black Gutter Bottom, Hampton Ridge, Latchmore, Cooper's Hill all without a car in sight but a paradise of tracks for walkers and riders. No wonder there is a greater number of stables up here than anywhere else in the Forest, so we visited Arniss Stables down a long, narrow lane among low-lying green meadows where horses grazed, the land rising all round to sheltering trees.

The name Arneys was recorded in the New Forest perambulation of 1218 and was originally a farm. The present house is about a hundred years old. The Great Barn, now carefully restored, and the stable blocks form three sides of the yard, a compact and charming picture with the afternoon ride getting ready to move off. There were sixteen horses at livery (boarders, that is). We met Arabel, the eventer, Louise, an Arab, Archie, a palomino stallion, and Saladin who specialized in dressage, in the cleanest and tidiest range of stables we had ever seen, the new buildings carefully designed to stand in harmony with the old brick and tile barns.

Two magpies cased the sawdust of the training ring: the string of riders was distant now, climbing toward Hampton Ridge and freedom without setting hoof to tarmac. Three rides go out on weekdays, but Saturdays and Sundays the stable works flat out through the hours of daylight.

Opposite Arniss Lane stands the entrance to Sandy Balls, the odd name given to the small, round, sandy hills which occur here along the 200-foot contour line.

Thomas Westlake came to nearby Fordingbridge in 1843 to work in his uncle's sailcloth business at East Mills: it was his son Ernest who bought Sandy Balls in 1919, intending to preserve its natural beauty but also to use it as a camping ground for the Order of Woodcraft Chivalry which he had recently founded, and for Forest School Camps which have now spread all over Britain.

The people of Godshill Street had for centuries cut faggots for their ovens and fires here, and that right remains to them. They had also dipped water from the springs, till Aubrey Westlake installed pumps and the first standpipes with taps for the village in the 1930s. Fifty years later, Westlakes still run Sandy Balls, still make nature and camping work together. Once inside, our first impression was of a pleasant site, caravans spaced out under mature trees, but really one needs a whole day to explore.

We walked north first through pine woods to see the heronry; but no birds circled the larches so early in the year. Eight pairs nested in 1982 but the numbers have declined though it would seem an ideal site high above the Avon. Here we could just glimpse through the winter trees the imposing turfy ramparts of Godmans Cap Camp, on private ground, said to be the largest defensive camp in the Forest. Dating from neolithic times, its eleven enclosed acres would have been a refuge for all the tribe and their animals in time of danger.

Below us secluded Ram Valley is kept as a nature reserve where badgers roam out at twilight through the first green points of wood sorrel and golden saxifrage, all undisturbed under the beeches.

We walked south through various kinds of camp site, from permanent home to tent space. (Sandy Balls holds the coveted Rose Award given by the English Tourist Board to only forty holiday parks in Britain), but in between are water-meadows, a sawmill, Folk House, festive circle, Duck House, quiet glades for family graves – an extraordinary mix.

Folk dances used to be held in the Great Barn at Arniss, but since that is now stabling, the dances have moved up to Sandy Balls.

At the southern end of the estate we came to Good Friday Hill, a sandy knoll covered with pines, sloping so steeply to the river that we were actually looking down on the lower treetops. Here an old Godshill custom has been revived, the rolling of decorated, hard-boiled eggs down the slope every Easter with prizes for those that roll farthest. This used to be a widespread custom on Easter Day: at Godshill, just to be different, it is always held on Good Friday.

Crossing the ford at Blissford, avoiding ponies in the windy lane, we came back to Frogham, another scattered hamlet, but it is worth pausing beside the Foresters Arms to look at the old barn. Alas, it is not a thing of beauty with the roof fallen in, but the sandy-coloured walls remain, a fine example of traditional dob or cob. Here on the edge of the forest, land was often acquired by squatters' rights, and the cheapest way to build was by using free materials to hand. Mud walls, or dob, were made of sand and clay mixed with small stones and quantities of chopped heather, rushes or straw – the mixing was done by trampling it all together. This was then shaped into walls with a three-tined mud prong, rearing about two feet, which had to be left to dry out thoroughly before the next layer was added. At Frogham you can see bracken stems mixed in the mud for strengthening.

We have returned full circle to our vantage point above Latchmore, old gravel pits now used as a car-park, this time to walk up Latchmore Bottom into real forest, for until now we have been exploring the forest edge, a gentle pastoral landscape with its own charm but not typical of the real forest.

A track leads down into the valley and a wide stretch of green lawn by the brook where three ponies are grazing, brown and sturdy, taking no notice of us. This is Latchmore Shade, a name peculiar to the New Forest, having nothing to do with trees. Here, out in the middle of the open lawn where some breeze circulates, dozens of ponies will gather on summer days, whisking the flies from each other, by standing in pairs, head to tail, conserving energy until evening brings cooler airs and they wander off to graze. There are many shades, or cool places in the forest, most of them on higher ground and often by water such as Ocknell Pond.

On our left, heathland slopes up toward Hampton Ridge, the old heather purple-brown like brush heads, but gorse brightening the air even in chill February. The brook loops round grassy banks, a clear brown over gravel, or slips through tussocky bog; boots are essential to the enjoyment of a forest walk, even in summer. The track more or less disappears but it has brought us to the great woods of Sloden.

A fallen oak makes a rough bridge over the stream, throws the water into eddies and a deep pool under a bank green with hard fern; a hazel droops yellow catkins over the water, and a grey squirrel leaps away at our approach, leaving his pile of acorns. Huge oaks and a few pines spread up the hillside with an understorey of holly. Woodspurge and foxglove leaves show above the leaf litter, too acrid for the deer to browse off. Coming to a wide driftway between inclosure and Sloden Wood, we find a small herd of fallow feeding, one of them a pale sandy colour which will mature into white; otherwise all is still, not a bird sings and all the leaves are fallen.

Strange to think then that this hillside was once a scene of busy workers humping clay, searching for wood, loading up orders. Sloden is one of many forest sites where pottery was made by Romanized Britons, not just for local use but to supply

Roman army posts all over the country. Heywood Sumner excavated four kilns, finding several perfect terracotta pots now in the British Museum. Nettles, which do not normally grow here, mark the disturbed ground of old excavations.

Sloden Wood covers the further hillside, bare old oaks wide spaced, and whitebeam, its silvery leaves contrasting in summer with the bottle-green of yew, both unusual trees. Many of the yews are dead or dying, no one can discover why. It can hardly be old age considering the many venerable churchyard yews. Sloden has a brooding, ancient air: ivy stems, or drums, thick as a thigh, snake round an ash planted the year of Waterloo.

We retrace our steps along the ruts of an old fern track. Bracken, or fern, used to be cut from the end of August, a ticket being obtained first from the Forestry Commission, three shillings a wagon load, before the last war, or half price after 26 September. The fern was cut in squares by scythe, raked together with a fork and stood on to press it down: some sixty of these bundles, called pooks, made up a wagon load. They were left to dry out for several days, then piled into ricks which were then thatched with rushes; later it was used to cover hobs (clamps) of potatoes or mangolds, to bed down a sow and her litter, in fact anywhere that straw is now used. After the straw-bailer came into general use, it was no longer economic to cut fern. A few commoners still cut small amounts as bedding for ponies, but the great piled wagons no longer creak homeward along Latchmore Bottom.

A side effect of cutting the fern, often tall as a man, was to make the woods more accessible. Towards the end of her life, Mrs Gaskell came to live in Hampshire. The heroine of her novel *North and South*, Margaret, goes sketching in the woods. 'When the brilliant days of October came on, she thought of nothing but the glories of the forest. The fern harvest was over and many a deep glade accessible into which Margaret had only peeped in July.'

Back at the gravel pits we returned to the border road and Hyde, a small village spread round a wide, gorsy common. The Victorian school building is still in use, exuberant portraits in poster colours visible through the windows – perhaps the next generation of mural painters. The other side of the common is dominated by the twin bell turret of the church, a chapel-like building erected in 1850 on a shelf above the Avon, like Hale in position, but here the river view is blocked by the dark leaves of rioting evergreens.

Though nowhere in the forest is really high, Hyde has an airy, upland feeling about it; perhaps the quality of the air accounts for the success of Hyde Band, which has been playing for nearly a hundred years now except for breaks in the wars. Many of the early players were local farm workers who would bike to practise with their instruments strapped on their backs! Their very first engagement was to play for Queen Victoria's Jubilee in 1897. Today, with a repertoire ranging from pop to classics, they take part in many championships besides being in great demand for the summer shows that are so flourishing in all the forest villages. Currently the age range is from nine to seventy.

A short hill brings us down to river level at North Gorley, a few cottages, the Royal Oak pub and a café strung along a green beside the road, low-lying and inclined to be marshy, with a stream along its far side and a pond in the middle. For a long time this was grown in with willow and reeds, but recently the village got together, cleared the scrub and encouraged ducks to move in, so that it is now a pretty feature with mallards preening on the bank, a moorhen skittering for cover in its shy way.

Further along the road, South Gorley is another scattered hamlet; the green this time is triangular, with donkeys grazing. Gorley was for nearly forty years the home of Heywood Sumner, a much-loved New Forest figure, writer, artist and archaeologist. He actually trained as a lawyer but never practised, showing great talent in drawing and etching. Becoming involved with William Morris and the Arts and Crafts movement, he published his first book in 1881 illustrated with etchings of the Itchen valley. He also designed windows and mosaics for churches.

By 1897 Sumner was living in Bournemouth with his wife and five children but determined to find a country home where they could settle down. Looking round Gorley one day, he found the perfect site on the hill above. 'I had quite decided that Cuckoo

Hill was the place that I wanted.' There was a tumbledown, mud-walled cottage in the field, which, after haggling, he bought for £175 – other fields called Paradise he added later. He designed the house to look down over Ibsley Common, which came in very useful. 'The Common supplied shingle for concrete, gravel for the road and paths, yellow and silver sand for the mortar and rough cast. Bricks from Deacon at Blissford at thirty three and sixpence a thousand and delivered here.'

At Cuckoo Hill he wrote *The Book of Gorley*, now scarce and valuable. This ranged over the whole forest and even Cranborne Chase as well as the village below and its people. From it comes this description of moving in.

'The vans were delayed on the road and didn't reach Gorley till four o'clock. Then they stuck in the clay on the hill – immovably. There was nothing to be done but to unload them there. So Peggy, our old white pony, was put in the cart and all the workmen in the job and everyone in Gorley came to help; and then by the light of a frosty moon and of stable lanthorns, our household goods were conveyed in long and repeated processions to the unfurnished house.'

In his years at Gorley, Heywood Sumner devoted himself to writing, drawing and archaeology. *Ancient Earthworks of the New Forest* was published in 1917, other books covered the Sloden potteries, Rockbourne and Cranborne, but his best-known book must be *A Guide to the New Forest*, 1923 and still in print, illustrated with his beautifully detailed black and white drawings.

Today Cuckoo Hill is a Home for the Elderly, its outside little changed – double-gabled, pebble-dashed with a glass turret on the roof and large windows looking down across pretty terraced gardens. The owners cherish the memory of Heywood Sumner – a happy house they say – and were delighted to find some original William Morris wallpaper during alterations. A photograph of Heywood Sumner looks out over the elegant drawing-room he designed.

Ibsley, under the sweep of Ibsley Common, is the place to do your shopping! Not that there is a shop in sight along the road but smallholdings sell home-grown beef, lamb and brown eggs at their gates, market gardens advertise lettuce, spring onions, new potatoes in their season, while others invite you to pick your own strawberries and currants. Here the pond has not been improved, its verge a trampled sea of mud – but it is full of frog spawn.

According to the map, this low-lying road through wet fields and scattered bungalows is just inside the Forest, yet it seems tamed, flat, a different world from deep woods, wild heathlands. These are never far away though. A turn to the left brings us under Rockford Common, a great sweep of heathery hillside patched with bracken and birches that might be an outpost of Dartmoor. Soon we turn into Appleslade Inclosure to watch the forest at work.

First we pass an open space littered with dead branches, a few mature beech trees left dotted about. It is Forestry Commission policy never to clear fell now: twenty per cent of the trees are left always so that the lands will not seem too bare and stripped. Then, if they care so much for the look of the land, why don't they clear up all this dead brash and get on with re-planting, we thought. Look again – something green amongst all the dead twigs, and there, and there, as the eye picks up a line. The whole clearing is planted with Douglas fir, three years old now, a foot high, the old branches left to afford them some protection against squirrel and deer. The new wood will have its first thinning-out when twenty-five years old.

Deeper into the inclosure we are surrounded by towering grey-barked Corsican pine, Norway spruce and Scots pine with its coppery trunks. Line-thinning is in progress, and great piles of felled timber line the track, most of it Douglas fir with orange heart wood, a strong, coarse wood, ideal for building construction. This was an order for a builder's merchant, all the wood being bought on site before it is felled.

The felling gang was only two men, with chainsaws and a tractor. They wore special padded trousers and leather boots with steel toe-caps. Even so, Jim, who was about to fell an enormous Douglas fir, had just caught the edge of his chainsaw in a thick ivy runner so that it dropped on his foot, chewing right through the leather and even his sock before he could get it clear, though he was unhurt.

It was important for the tree to fall away from a young plantation where it could do much damage, so the sink, or wedge, was taken out with the saw on the opposite side – Jim and his mate reckoned they could drop a tree along a piece of string. This one was forty-six years old, measured at breast height for size. The next thinning would be in five years time, giving the wild life of the wood time to recover.

With a rumble like distant thunder, the fir landed exactly where Jim had wanted it, shaking the ground beneath our feet. He would fell up to twenty-five trees in a day. His mate painted the stump with a bright blue fungicide to stop fungus colonizing it and spreading to live trees. Jim measured the trunk with a tape kept clipped to his belt, then they shedded out – that is, took off the branches. When only the trunk was left, one end was chained to the winch on the tractor and it was dragged out to the main stack.

Further along stood a pile of very long logs, peeled of their bark. These were telegraph poles ordered by British Telecom, who pay well but only for a high grade of tree fitting exact measurements. They must be cut by the end of February before the sap begins to rise. Other 'tall orders' are for ships' masts and flagpoles.

A forwarder growled into view, a tractor with four wheels each side, holding a cage and a big grab crane for loading up timber. Five or six were chained together, then lifted by the grab into the cage, which could hold six tons. This order was going to Sunbury on Thames to make hardboard. Some go as far afield as mid Wales, others to local mills to be used eventually as dock piles, fencing panels and football posts, while lower-grade soft wood makes fruit crates and cardboard.

It is surprising in fact to learn that seven lorry loads of timber leave the forest *every day*, and all this, the real work of the Forestry Commission, has to be balanced with our pleasure as walkers, commoners' rights, the well-being of donkey and deer, fern and foxglove, and with all the other activities going on here – camping, riding and field study, for example.

Every now and then we had come across signs of badgers in the woods, a paw print, fresh droppings in Sloden: now we crossed into Roe Inclosure and its environs to check on activity there. On the edge of the wood among fir, oak and bramble flitted parties of tits, long-tailed, blue and tiny coal tits. By Linford Bridge we are in the heart of the wood: great oaks spread away on all sides above a sea of fox-coloured bracken that seems to light the air, and all is still. On our right we can glimpse the broken bank of Castlepiece, a pre-Roman circle thrown up to make a place of refuge for people and cattle alike.

Through a gate and in splendid contrast here is rolling grassland bracken, gorse and wide horizons, a re-seeded area called King's Garden, perhaps originally King's Bee Garden. For hundreds of years hives have been brought out onto the heathlands for summer to give the bees freedom of acres of ling and bell heather: honey was once the only sweetener available, but its chief use in these parts, as at Woodgreen, was in making mead, a drink some four times more powerful than beer and often used to lace it. Beekeepers still bring out their bees, paying a fee to the Forestry Commission for the privilege, so from July to September King's Garden will be home to bees from Fairoak, near Portsmouth.

A wide hillside sloping gently down to Milkham Inclosure, patched with gorse and old ling bushes three feet high, is home to voles, rabbits and small birds such as stonechats and pippits – which in turn makes good feeding ground for predators. Here in winter hen-harriers come hunting, in size between kestrel and buzzard, gliding in low, intent to pounce, silvery winged or black-barred chestnut, for male and female are extraordinarily unalike; often three or four will roost together.

Down in a nearby inclosure the streamside lawn is a brighter green than most winter grass, for when the stream floods its bank rich silt is deposited on the lawn, giving the plants extra nourishment – no wonder a herd of ponies, chestnut and black, are grazing it with concentration. Here in the inclosure bank, under beeches and ferns but looking out over lawns, is a really enormous badger sett, bare humpy ground stretching for fifty yards along the kind of 'frontier' site they like best, pitted with old fallen-in holes. New holes are marked by piles of fresh sandy soil, and mats of bracken, old bedding thrown out before new was taken down, clasped in the badger's paws, in readiness for the cubs to be born.

Even tonight there will be little activity round the sett: the males may come out to forage for a short time but the females will stay below, suckling their cubs. Badgers mate in July and August though the embryos do not start to grow at any speed for some five months. The cubs are born blind, about five inches long, two or three to a litter, and will not come above ground for at least six weeks – even then they are very shy, peering short-sightedly from the setts' sheltering mouth at the wide world beyond. By summer they will be bolder, even coming out before their parents and romping together in the twilight. We found ourselves talking in whispers, and as we crept away from the setts it was good to remember that the nursing mothers below and their cubs were protected in the forest and could not be trapped or dug out. They are widespread, do little harm and help keep the rabbit population within bounds.

All through Sloden and Appleslade, Roe Wood and Linford we had walked through ancient and beautiful woods in the winter quiet, disturbed only by a robin's trill, a rabbit's thumper alarm, for all the tracks in this part of the forest are open only to Forestry Commission vehicles, the gates padlocked and bearing a small notice 'Car Free Area'.

This is only one of the far-ranging changes brought about in the early 1970s. By the end of the sixties it had become plain the forest was threatened on all sides. Indiscriminate camping, parking, riding and driving were eroding commons and heaths: everywhere visitors were destroying the very countryside they had come to enjoy. The problem seemed so desperate there was even talk of enclosing the entire New Forest and making one pay to enter it! Instead, a working party was set up with representatives from the Forestry Commission, Hampshire County Council, the Nature Conservancy, the Verderers and the Rural District Councils of Ringwood, Fordingbridge and the New Forest. They eventually produced a report, 'Conservation of the New Forest' – a fat collection of charts, maps, photographs and possible solutions, a most interesting read for anyone who loves the forest, not at all the dry legal document you might expect.

The report recommended the creation of twenty-six car-free zones, with more car-parks and access points for walkers. Everyone who cherishes the real forest atmosphere must be grateful that these suggestions were put into practice so that one can wander all day free from exhaust fumes and grinding gears.

Linwood is a widely scattered hamlet little known to visitors unless they seek out Red Shoot Inn or the pub at High Corner. You have to negotiate a long, gravelly track to find this picturesque jumble of buildings, some of them dating back to early 1700s – here you are really enclosed by forest, yet there's a squash court for the energetic, also family rooms and a woodland garden. The home cooking really is delicious, including game pie and venison sausage. Otherwise Linwood is a quiet scatter of smallholdings, stables and farms, fields and woods between the high forest of Milkham and the valley of Dockens Water. Here we went to see Eric Ashby, the first man to film badgers underground in the wild, who showed us how it was done.

The badgers originally lived in a big old sett on the edge of a copse at the bottom of a field adjoining his house. Drainpipes were laid through a bank at the top end leading into a 'sett' specially dug out and covered with a great heap of earth. From this more pipes led into two more badger living-rooms, but these are cunningly placed beside a shed with observation windows in the side. When all this was ready, trails of food, bread, household scraps and acorns soon led the copse badgers to the bank. With surprising speed they found the new home and have been using it ever since.

Today there was no one in, since it is breeding time and they have not yet used it to have their young, but bring the cubs on visits as soon as they are old enough: only a large pile of bracken awaited any badger wanting a quiet snooze. On a previous visit we had crept into the shed at night and sat entranced in total darkness, watching the badgers through the glass panels in their lit chambers.

We were just in time to see the rear end of a young badger disappearing down the tunnel, the long hanging fur giving a kilted effect, but looking out of the shed's back window we could see, in the moonlight, another moving purposefully up the field. Soon she appeared in the lit sett, suspicious at first, sniffing round the walls, then, scenting food, she went through to the last chamber. Here food was laid out in three bowls. With her piglike, slightly upturned snout, she sniffed the first, then the second and finally decided the third was the tastiest meal, rooting about amongst the bread for fragments of stale pie but finally eating the lot, her fears forgotten.

She was a sow in the prime of life, the long black and white hairs of her coat so well groomed they gleamed silver, small, neat ears rimmed with black, small, short-sighted eyes giving her a shy expression, and fearsome black claws. The black and white face seemed once or twice turned enquiringly towards the glass panel while we held our breath, moved with wonder at being so close to a wild creature at home.

Down another winding Linwood lane we visited a forest farm. Here an open yard with covered stalls on three sides was full of black and white Friesians – there are 112 all together, though the milking herd was out in the fields around. These were the dry cows who had looked in for their breakfast of concentrates. As they finished their nuts, they turned around, left the yard and wandered back up the lane to the common where they would browse around till next morning, once more returning unbidden for their daily snack. They get this supplementary feed right through from September to April.

At the moment it costs £10 a year to turn a beast out on the forest, though farmers with Adjacent Commons Rights can send out a percentage at cheaper rates.

The unwanted calves from this farm are sold at Salisbury Market, which offers better prices than Ringwood on the whole. Calves are never bought at Salisbury though: animals reared on Wiltshire chalk land do not thrive if brought onto the forest, so stock is bred on the premises. Ringwood Market has declined as the number of smallholders has decreased. As at Woodgreen, the desirability of a New Forest cottage has pushed the price of property beyond the reach of local people, especially young married couples.

The last cow ambled past on its way up to the common, and

we turned down the lane to journey into the past.

For the Romans and their descendants were busy here too. In a private woodland garden six pottery kilns have been excavated, and the fine pots which were found can now be seen in the Red House Museum at Christchurch. For us the excitement lay in what the experts had left behind. Scrabbling among dead leaves in the still wintry wood we came upon a heap of pottery fragments, matchbox size or smaller. Under a hazel, a rabbit had dug a new burrow in the sand-coloured earth – and turned up black soil. Crumbling it in your fingers, you could smell the charcoal used to fire these kilns sixteen hundred years ago ... At the copse edge a badger had scraped after beetles, and just showing under the broad paw mark was a curve of handle. A little digging unearthed the slender neck of a jar, deep-lipped to pour wine. Elsewhere, among the primrose tumps, lay half a lid, such as we still use on a casserole, a thumb-sized fragment bearing a scratch pattern like trellis work, a pot rim with an ancient thumb mark.

J.R. Wise, writing a hundred years ago, described a kiln he had excavated in Oakley Inclosure: 'It was circular and measured six yards in circumference, its shape being well defined by small, handformed masses of red brick-earth. The floor, about two feet below the natural surface of the ground was paved with a layer of sandstone.' The pottery itself is coarse, rough and dingy even when cleaned up but this in no way detracted from the interest of this industrial estate of long ago: we could happily have spent days there hunting for larger fragments or trying to piece the smaller ones together, frequently helped in our search by archaeologizing rabbits, who would prefer not to know about our next visit.

The cottage lay a mile down a rough, potholed track, surrounded by burgeoning vegetable gardens – and sheds ranged with hutches full of ferrets at every stage, white furred babies with bright pink noses, eyes still shut, half-grown kits like cuddly toys except for their already sharp claws, and full-grown animals, both ordinary white and the more handsome brown polecat cross. With a terrier and nets they were used to hunt rabbits in winter months, on private land.

'This one'll turn up a dozen rabbits in an hour,' said its owner, fondly stroking the hank of fur curled around his neck.

We walked back over Rockford Common, one of the few high, undulating tracks of heath, with old heather and bracken underfoot, larks and pippits springing up, gorse bushes beloved of yellowhammers in summer. From the top we could see north and west across Linwood Bog and Ibsley Common to the valley of Dockens Water and vast, rolling heathland stretching away toward Cranborne Chase, with the pines of Whitefield Plantation darkly silhouetted against a sunset sky on the next ridge.

The shallower undulations are in fact worked-out sandpits, long disused and grassed over, but the summit path leads us to something much deeper – the land climbs and narrows to a jutting prow, a lone pine tree, then falls sharply away in steep cliffs, into a vast pit. While it was still being worked, sand martens nested here in burrows; now that it is disused but accessible to walkers, they have, sad to say, deserted it.

From the lone pine we looked out over acres of shining water, the gravel pits at Blashford, large enough to support a yacht club. Beyond them through the trees the Avon gleamed, flowing down to Ringwood, where the church tower made an unmistakable landmark.

Ringwood is just outside the forest boundary but many of the smaller farms and holdings still use its market; there are other links too, so we felt bound to explore the town, choosing Wednesday which has been market day ever since Henry III granted its charter in 1226.

The earliest form of name was Rincveda, changed to Rinkewode by the thirteenth century. In the Domesday survey it was assessed at 'nothing', almost all the manor having been taken into the New Forest – which *was* new then. Nevertheless, there were frequent squabbles as to ownership; at one time it was granted to Simon de Steyland for the yearly rent of one sore sparrowhawk. Later it passed through various famous owners, all of whom met violent ends, Warwick the Kingmaker, killed in the Battle of Barnet, Edward Plantagenet, beheaded for helping Perkin Warbeck's conspiracy, and Sir John Gates, the King's favourite steward, who died for helping Lady Jane Grey.

The manor tenants had common rights in the New Forest among the knights and squires, for their farm and plough beasts, and for all stock except goats and geese, though they had also to render service such as mowing the lord of the manor's meadows, helping with haymaking and carting and with the repair of houses and mills, of which there were several on the Avon.

Thomas Lyne was an early benefactor, giving his farm tithes at Burley, in 1621, to send a poor scholar from Ringwood Free School to Oxford or Cambridge for four years on an annuity of £6 a year; in fact Ringwood was quite famous for the number of its charities.

In 1974 the manor was sold to the Morant family of Brockenhurst, whom we shall meet again. ('Manor' here, as often in this book, means the whole estate, rather than just a house.) They took a great interest in the town, building a town hall and a theatre. By this time Ringwood was becoming industrial, with trade in leather and cloth, a collar and cuff factory, three sawmills with various wheelwrights and furniture-makers all using wood out of the forest, and a thriving cottage industry making stockings and gloves. A guidebook of 1940 refers to 'Ringwoods' still being made, white woollen gloves once very fashionable with young men.

Locally its most famous product was Ringwood Ale, dispensed from twenty inns and brewed by the Carter family in West Street – they boasted a 5,000-gallon vat in which the annual party was held! Their tied houses included the Queen's Head at Burley and the Horse and Groom at Woodgreen. The brewery has gone, but Malt Houses remain in Duck Island Lane.

Perhaps to counteract the effects of too much strong ale, acres of land off Hightown Road were planted with camomile, which was made into medicines to settle the stomach – camomile tea is still used in this way, and the flowers are sometimes used in bath sachets.

The Wednesday crowd, dressed functionally in 'wellies' and head scarves or caps, swept us along toward the market. Most of the town is built of bricks in a distinctive shade of rust red;

these were made locally at Bransgore, Hightown and Verwood, and their warm colour, together with roofscapes of old tiles, crooked chimneys and dormers, gives the town a certain homely charm in spite of all the new shop fronts. We paused outside the White Hart, Ringwood's best-known pub, to admire its signboard, a white deer wearing a gold collar, and to read the legend beneath.

When Henry VII, the Archduke Philip, Joan his Spanish wife and many lords and ladies went hunting in the forest, a famous hart known as Albert gave them such a fine run that, when he finally stood at bay by the Avon, the ladies of the party interceded, so the hounds were called off and Albert was led into Ringwood. After being given a gold collar, he was removed to Windsor, while Halliday Wagstaffe, Keeper of Woods and Forests, was knighted in the town. The house where King and courtiers took their refreshment was christened 'the White Hart'.

Nearly three centuries later, George III used to break his journey at the same pub when travelling through Hampshire, admiring crowds watching him quaff that powerful Ringwood Ale from a quart tankard.

The church with its battlemented tower is nineteenth century, very light and spacious inside, with three tall lancet windows in glowing jewel colours at the east end, in memory of John Morant, Lord of Ringwood, 1857.

Market Place is flanked by the church, new shops, a glimpse of thatch, old cottages and some fine Georgian town houses, though on Wednesday morning all the activity is out in the middle. Stalls sell fish, anoraks, boxes of plants, plastic trains, brassware, pork chops, saddles, but what distinguishes it from ordinary street markets is the number of auctions taking place – at the moment the crowd is thickest round a produce stall where the auctioneer is holding up a bag of oranges and inviting bids. Behind him a whole collection of second-hand machines awaits the next auction, several lawnmowers, three vacuum cleaners and a fridge, while a very old bike leans against the ornate lamp standard, now painted purple, erected to celebrate Queen Victoria's Jubilee, in 1887.

Leaving the market hubbub behind, we walked down a quiet street past sixteenth-century cottages and Monmouth House,

A Breath of Fresh Air: Beech woodland

Sowley Pond

(*Opposite*) Furzey Gardens, the pond

Eyeworth Pond

Tidal Mill, Beaulieu

Autumn at the Queen's Head, Burley

where that rebel was brought captive after being defeated at the Battle of Sedgemoor and wrote his abject letters to James II – all in vain. This brought us to a delightful little corner, Jubilee Gardens, recently laid out on a curve of the Avon, lawns and benches, lime trees bending over a footbridge and the old three-arched stone bridge, boys fishing for dace, the river lip-lapping past – yes, in a way it is a peaceful haven, but the air vibrates all the time with the roar of traffic from the bypass, the building of which brought such chaos in the 1970s. On the other hand the town streets were busy only with local traffic; indeed, once everyone had fought their way into a parking space, it was not so traffic-ridden even on its busiest day. Back in Market Place bidding was brisk for a basket of cabbages.

Stanley Gibbons, the world famous stamp-dealers, have a branch here in a beautiful Georgian house. A path through the churchyard brings us to the yard of a sawmill where they use larch, out of the forest, and into the beast market, a collection of sheds in a large muddy yard surrounded by high old brick walls.

Everywhere little auctions were going on in corners, for a rabbit, a goat, or baskets of eggs in the egg shed. One pen held Gloucester Spot pigs, a rare breed now, but on the whole this is a homely, even old-fashioned market much used by the forest commoners. Ivy grew over one shed and a lawnmower had strayed among the poultry cages.

To be fair, Ringwood has moved with the times in other ways. Another elegant Georgian building houses a thriving Community Centre, while a pioneer in engineering, Armfields, gave rise to the big industrial estate on the town's edge.

Other buildings to search out are the Manor House, now separated by a road from its stable block with little tower and clock, and the alms houses in Quomp. At first sight the range of mellow brick gables and high chimneys appears to be Tudor (in the style of Hampton Court) but seems in suspiciously good repair. In fact, they were built in 1833, each house to be occupied by a married couple or two women, given 2s. 6d each per week.

Quomp is such an unusual name it is disappointing to find it otherwise an undistinguished road of old and new houses, though the collar and cuff factory stood here, and the camomile works. The word means, possibly, quiet place, or a marshy place, which seems more likely as it slopes toward the river, where the watercress beds used to be. (How tempting to think Quomp equals quiet swamp!)

As the only town on the western edge, Ringwood is shopping centre for a large area of the forest. One of the latest developments is in Meeting House Lane, where the eighteenth-century meeting house in old rust brick has been incorporated into a shopping precinct. Here, as in other of Ringwood's latest buildings, an attempt has been made to match up the rust colour of the bricks: the shops have been built in a covered cloister round a brick and beamed square once the Quakers' burial ground. Here old and new meet most curiously. 'Sale today' shouts an orange poster from a new shop window, while beside it stands a stone table tomb dated 1864.

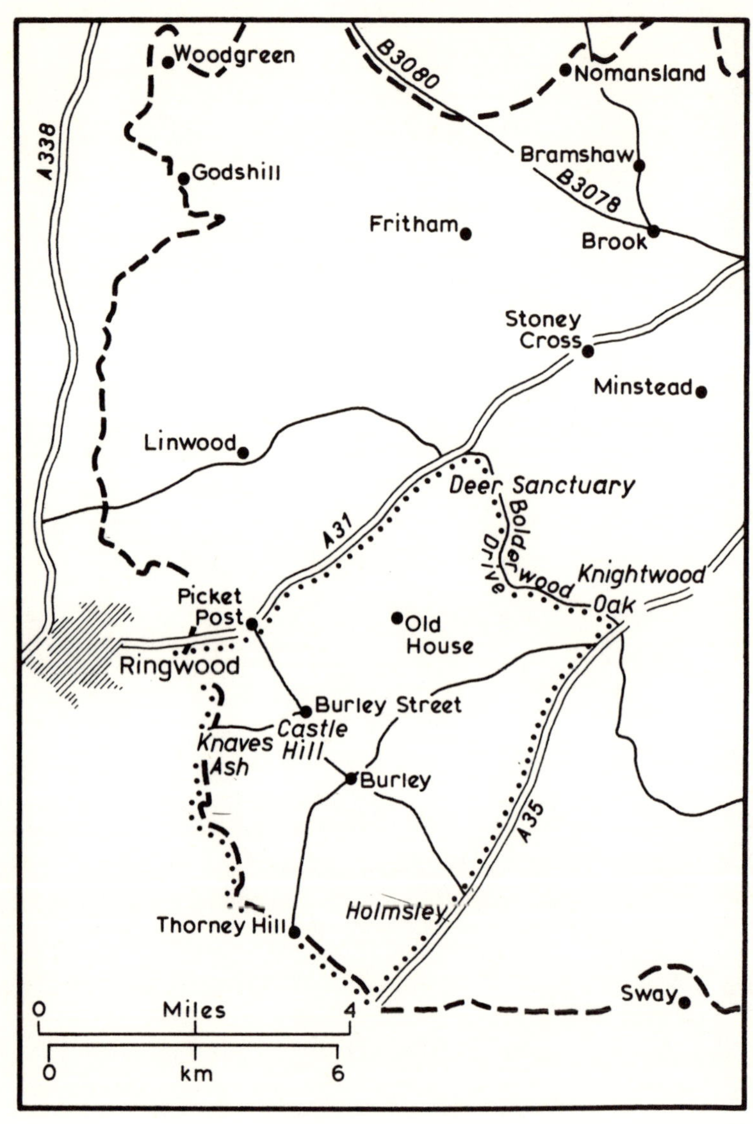

Burley and the South West

2 *Burley and the South West*

Douglas firs soar 150 feet above our heads, their rust-brown bark convoluted into great wrinkles thick as rope under graceful hanging branches, April sun dappling the brown forest floor with moving shadows of leaf and needle. We begin exploring the Burley area at Bolderwood.

The first tracks through the forest were made by woodcutters and charcoal-burners: the one nearby eventually became a carriage route from Brockenhurst to Ringwood and an entrance to Bolderwood Lodge. Many specimen conifers were planted in the grounds in 1860, and though the house has long been pulled down, its kitchen becoming a keeper's lodge, the trees have grown into the magnificent collection known now as Bolderwood Arboretum.

The forest track, adopted and surfaced in 1964, became Bolderwood Ornamental Drive, one of the most popular and accessible areas, well served with car-parks, waymarked paths, information leaflets. To the thousands of town-dwellers who come to the New Forest as to a new land, it is reassuring to be told that a particular walk will take half an hour and that following the green flashes will bring you back to the car-park.

Following no particular route, we wandered down through the tall firs and came upon the Radnor Memorial, a slate slab beautifully carved with forest wildlife, owl and crossbill, fallow deer and squirrel, oak, beech, bluebell and many more. The Earl of Radnor was a Forestry Commissioner for many years, and Official Verderer in the 1960s: near his stone stand little groups of young trees planted by various local schools in 1969 – Jubilee Grove – to mark the fiftieth anniversary of the Forestry Commission.

On the hill above, young trees crowd close, shutting out the sun. These are Douglas fir, sprung naturally from cast cones, which will eventually be thinned out, to grow into new giants.

In the arboretum each special tree is numbered so that with leaflet in hand you can identify the silvery bark of Corsican pine, much grown in the forest, or the more exotic – swamp cypress from America, Japanese cedar, Chile pine, Italian poplar. Perhaps the redwood from California is the most striking of all, with its bright orange-brown trunk, hairy as a coconut, 130 feet tall.

As we pottered along broad paths through this sunny green world, turning down any track which seemed inviting, listening to the monotonous song of a chiff-chaff, we came upon a man watching a crossbill attack a fallen pine cone and pull out the seeds – nothing odd you might think, but the man in the middle of a wood was in a wheelchair.

Bolderwood is one of the forest areas specially designed for the disabled, and indeed those with prams or pushchairs: there are other such sites at Hatchet Pond, Wilverley and Linwood Bottom. Here the paths are smooth, of gentle gradient and graded short, middle and long walks, with a specially wide kissing gate to make easy access from the car-park. Not everyone wants to tramp the wilds of Sloden. A gentle meander through the magnificent trees of Bolderwood must be just the tonic for anyone convalescent and long housebound. The various narrator posts are all set at easy reading height from a wheelchair.

Quietly we moved down the wooded slope and up wooden steps to the deer observation platform. Here an antler diagram shows how to recognize a pricket (one year old) from a sorel (two years old), and information boards give a brief history of the four breeds to be found in the forest, currently fifty red, six hundred fallow, sixty sika and three hundred and fifty roe – but more important than any of this, there were the deer themselves, a few yards away.

Though there has never been any attempt to tame them, some years ago a keeper began to throw down food in a field near Bolderwood Farm. Fallow deer soon took advantage of this, becoming regular visitors. One cannot guarantee they will be in sight: three days later there was not a hoof to be seen, but this morning we were lucky. In the field below was a herd of a dozen fallow buck, four of them grazing, the rest lying on the new sprung grass, drowsing in the sun. Two did rise slowly, stare at each other and finally clash antlers, but it was half hearted: they soon subsided back onto the grass. Two had already lost their antlers, as happens every April, one of them very recently as the bumps on his forehead were still red and sore-looking. Another scratched his ear, drowsed off.

1983 being the Year of the Disabled, the New Forest Association approached the Forestry Commission with the idea of modifying the deer observation platform for wheelchairs: this was done jointly and the new style platform officially opened in April 1983.

The longest of the waymarked walks led us into the Ancient and Ornamental woods and the great beeches of Mark Ash. Folly to choose the 'most beautiful' in the New Forest as Victorian writers often did, but these huge old trees wide spaced down a gentle slope, branches tipped with the first new green of spring, a white track winding enticingly away between tall silvery trunks – this must be *one* of the loveliest deciduous woods. Most of the beeches were pollarded when young, causing them to divide into a wide canopy of boughs parallel with the ground. Pollarding, or topping, was done to provide fuel and deer browse but was made illegal in 1698, which makes the Mark Ash beeches at least three hundred years old.

So it is not surprising that fallen giants lie everywhere, left to provide homes for vole and wren, fern and fungus, all adding to the richness of forest life. Here and there self-sown young beeches have been fenced off to protect them from deer and squirrel – infant giants to ensure the future of Mark Ash.

A guidebook of 1876 says, 'Close to a gnarled oak with a beech tree at its back will be seen the well defined track of the charcoal burners. Leaving the charcoal fires with the rude hut of the watchman between us and the turnpike road, we cross a forest streamlet and Mark Ash may be said to begin.' Another old book provides a watercolour of the 'rude hut', a wigwam of poles covered with turf except for a hole at the top, surrounded by a rough palisade of branches to keep any beasts from knocking it down. Here lived the charcoal-burners, keeping a slow fire going under a roof of turves, watching twenty-four hours a day to ensure that it never burst into flame. Charcoal was an essential ingredient of gunpowder right up to the war of 1914.

Down through Mark Ash lies North Oakley Inclosure, part of a great tract of woodland, Anderwood, Beech Bed and South Oakley stretching away south toward Burley, splendid walking country and magical at night when tawny owls glide down from hollow oaks where they have slept the day, their wild cries menacing the forest, while little owl scream, as the deer, most likely fallow, steal about the rides with scarcely a sound, their white rumps conspicuous in the dark. Nightjars nest along the wood's edge in more open country, adding their strange whirring call to the night sounds in May and June.

You can often glimpse a fox trotting purposefully along the track to the nearest car-park, for they long ago learned to find easy pickings of crumbs and scraps in spite of the frequent notices for visitors bidding them take their litter home.

Returning to the Ornamental Drive and daylight, a short walk eastward brought us to the Knightswood Oak, famous for its size and age – nearly four hundred years old probably, but now sadly dying back, losing great limbs, a shadow of former splendour. After the laws against pollarding were rescinded in the early 1970s, the Forestry Commission pollarded six young beeches and six oaks nearby as an experiment. A light, irregular tapping betrayed a nuthatch at work on the gnarled bark of old Knightwood, and a jay flew off with a flash of blue wing feather.

As part of the celebrations for the ninth centenary of the New Forest, founded by William I in 1079, the Queen herself, arriving by horse-drawn coach, planted an oak. Nearby a great beech has fallen and the extent of its roots has been marked out with pegs – an enormous circle.

Bolderwood Drive has five car-parks, beautiful woodland to be enjoyed even from a car and various places of interest within a short walking distance – no country for the red deer we wanted to photograph, though, so we set off for quieter woods.

Red deer, largest of the four species to be found in the forest, are natives of Britain, though their numbers have fluctuated greatly over the years, and they are prey to poachers to this day. Their numbers declined in the seventeenth century. 'Portsmouth, 1670. There arrived about sixty stags, being a gift from the French King to his Majesty. They are gone from the New Forest, the place appointed for them.' Cobbett, riding through the forest in 1826, fulminated, 'Why, there are more deer bred in Richmond Park alone than would feed all the branches of the Royal Family. For what and for whom then are deer kept in the New Forest: and why an expense of hay farm, of sheds, of racks, of keepers of lodges … more money annually than would have given relief to all the starving manufacturers in the North.'

So he would have been delighted by the Deer Removal Act of 1851, brought about by the high poaching rate and the difficulty of reafforesting decaying woods, since deer browsed off all the young trees. Most of the deer were removed, but by the end of the century a few red had returned and begun to breed. In 1908 Lord Montagu released a stag and several does, ancestors of the herd to be found in the south-east of the forest. More recently, says the deer information board, a small herd escaped from the grounds of Old House and began to breed in the Burley area.

We set out for Old House, a dream-like experience. A narrow lane, easily missed, leads off from a car-park on the Burley road, winds through dark conifers, oaks just bursting into coppery leaf, deeper and deeper into the woods with only a pigeon crooning, a crow flapping away from his carrion lunch – miles from anywhere we felt, out in the wild, till the next bend brought us in sight of a lake, a Georgian mansion, Old House.

No one quite knows why there should be a house here at all. Old maps mark the spot 'encroachment': deeds go back to someone named Scquear who made his mark, being unable to write. A nineteenth-century print shows a huddle of ramshackle cottages. These were bought by Auberon Herbert and rebuilt in brick at the turn of the century: he was an eccentric reformer, writer and lover of the forest, sleeping on top of a tower under the stars, throwing great strawberry teas in summer open to whoever might come and collecting flint stones to further his remarkable theory that Stone Age man chipped them into human portraits. He detected three distinct races, inferring that the most evolved would have been 'strong, self controlled, thoughtful and gentle, keen and patient observers of nature and appreciative of natural beauty'. At least this makes one look at flint stones in a new light! Auberon, loving the forest, wished never to leave it and is buried a little distance from Old House, near the wood called Mouse's Cupboard.

So the present house, though elegant Georgian in style, was actually built in the 1960s, the bricks of the Herbert house being used to make high garden walls. On one side a sea of daffodils rippled in the April breeze, on the other mallards snoozed beside a lake hung with willows. A peacock showed off his tail against budding azaleas; camellias bloomed against the sun-warmed old bricks that form sheltered courtyards hung with wistaria – yet twenty years ago this was rough heath and bog like that outside the fence.

The long drive is a private road, but Old House garden is occasionally open to the public in spring – not to be missed. This new Old House and garden are the creation of Sir Dudley Forwood, Official Verderer of the New Forest for twelve years until 1982. Leaving the gate and back on the forest side of the fence, we came upon Sir Dudley's Ride. To commemorate his great services to the New Forest over many years, the Forestry Commission named this path in his honour in 1982: it runs between Berry Beeches and Berry Wood to Mill Lawn Brook.

As we walked down it toward Old House Bottom, we could see on the left the remains of a high deer fence. In 1962, concerned at the scarcity of red deer, Sir Dudley bought a small herd from Horsham, in Surrey, keeping them for a time in this wooded valley where they bred, but eventually took to the wild. There are about fifty in the forest now, of which we had not yet glimpsed so much as a hoofprint.

Two forest keepers reckoned the deer were around Cranes Moor area, advising us to scan the country from the top of Castle Hill, Burley: once the herd was located, we could move nearer.

A very rough track climbs up to 'The Castle', a hundred feet above the surrounding heathland, the end of a ridge hummocked with old gravel pits and ponds, patched with woodland, hiding a few houses set in wide grounds such as Castle Top, another garden sometimes open to the public. But not all the bumps and hollows were caused by quarrying gravel. The Castle is the remains of a pre-Roman earthwork, a camp within a circular bank, refuge for tribe and stock on an almost impregnable site, for the ground falls away steeply on three sides, and even the fourth, an extension of the ridge, would have been bare ground with good visibility.

While trees and diggings have long obscured the shape of ramparts and entrances, the view remains vast, a wide stretch of heathland curiously dotted with basin-shaped sandhills: covered with heather still winter dark, they resemble enormous Christmas puddings – any one of these sandhills could have hidden a herd of deer on its far side, but there were none in sight.

Where the plateau gravel has remained intact, little grows. It was interesting to follow a wind-contorted tree down to the base and notice how it has taken root in the sides of the old pits where the gravel layer has gone, revealing the more fertile clay. None of the trees appears of great age so it seems unlikely there would have been enough cover for a dragon in 1460.

The story tells how, 'Sir Moris Barkley, of Beverston, being a man of great strength and courage, in his tyme there was bread in Hampshire neere Bisterne a devouring Dragon, who doing much mischief upon men and cattel and could not be destroyed but spoiled many in attempting it, making his den neere unto a Beacon. This Sir Moris Barkley armed himself and encountered with it and at length overcam and killed it but died himself soone after.'

The further end of this ridge is called Burley Beacon: Sir Moris was a real person, his mother born in nearby Bisterne. So what nugget of truth is the basis for this rewrite of our patron saint? Felicity Hardcastle, historian of Burley, suggests that the dragon was in fact the last wolf to haunt the neighbourhood. Wolves became extinct in England during Henry VII's reign – that is, after 1485, their last refuges being Wales and Scotland, so it seems feasible they could already have been very scarce in southern England by 1460, the date of Sir Moris's death.

Vainly hoping to glimpse deer on the way, we moved north to the hamlet of Picket Post. From the viewpoint car-park there is a fine panorama south-east right across the forest and the Solent to the downs of the Isle of Wight, though if they appear too close it means rain.

Motorists on the A31 could be forgiven for thinking Picket Post merely the place where there is a garage on either side of the road, though older drivers will remember another landmark, the Copper Kettle tea rooms with a big kettle hanging outside. But Picket Post has a past. Like Godshill it was known as a wild, lawless place, home for smugglers, poachers and squatters. Girls left pregnant by soldiers hurrying off to the Napoleonic Wars sought refuge there because, again like Godshill, Picket Post was an extra-parochial district. If they had applied to a parish for aid, they would have been sent back to the parish of their birth and ended up in the poorhouse.

The pub itself was encroached – that is, illegally built – on forest land and eventually became so rowdy it was closed down and turned into a tea house, the Copper Kettle. Lord Lucan, known as Bron, the son of Auberon Herbert, was a great character who founded the Burley and District Pony and Cattle Society, lost a leg in the Boer War but wangled his way into the Royal Flying Corps in 1914. He built a mansion here called Picket Post House which was used after his death as a boys' prep school during the last war. Afterwards it became a hotel but did not prosper: it was largely destroyed by a great fire. Insurance investigators found this had been started deliberately, and the owner went to prison for fraud. The ruins of Picket Post House and the Copper Kettle itself both disappeared when the A31 was made into a dual carriageway. What stories lie beneath that tarmac!

All is respectability now: in quiet lanes away from the main road secluded houses stand in spacious spring gardens. But still the view of heath and woodland revealed no red deer, so we took the western bye-road from Burley to Knaves Ash on the edge of the forest.

Just as Mark Ash, in all probability a tree marking a boundary, is now said to be a highwayman, so Knaves Ash is said to be named from a tree standing at the crossroads where criminals were hanged. We hardly cared, for here, not on wild moor or hidden in deep woods but sensibly eating the lush grass of an enclosed field, were the red deer, too intent on their delicious grazing to take any notice of us, though we were screened from them only by a straggly thorn hedge.

This was a stag herd, a splendid sight at any time but not in April at its stately best. Each had shed his antlers and was in process of moulting the thick brown winter coat which gave him a spotted, rather moth-eaten look: some bore patches of dried mud on their backs from wallowing in some boggy patch to loosen the old fur. But soon two furry bumps will appear on the forehead, developing quickly through the summer to velvet-clad antlers and the summer coat appears, sleek red-brown. By the autumn the antlers are full grown and stripped of their velvet, the herd breaks up and each stag goes off to round up a harem of hinds, rolling in his own urine and droppings mixed with mud to make himself the more desirable! At this time the forest will be rent with wild bellowings and clashing of antler as each stag defends his own territory and fights off intruding young males.

All this fighting and mating leaves little time for grazing, and when the rutting season is over, a stag will be many pounds thinner, so he must concentrate on eating well before hard weather sets in – his winter coat is beginning to grow.

We did not see a hind herd at this time. Wherever it was, each hind would be temporarily leaving the herd to seek out a secluded place for her calf, to be born in June. A calf's coat speckled with white spots is well camouflaged in dappled forest sunlight and indeed its only protection for the first few days, when its mother leaves it alone for most of the day, returning only three or four times to feed it, but in less than a week it is up and running, staying with its mother for a year, till the birth of the next calf and sometimes after that. A stag calf will grow his first antler bumps, or pedicles, the following spring. These will grow into mere spikes up to six inches long; each year the antlers should increase in size until the stag is at his prime at the age of about twelve, then as he ages they may begin to decrease.

Red deer are not hunted in the New Forest, but what would the farmer think of this herd grazing his best pasture? It is more often in winter that they come trampling onto farmland in search of food, earning themselves a bad reputation.

Knaves Ash, this thin scatter of houses where three lanes meet, was once an important junction on the smugglers' routes, and here by the crossroads lived the famous Warne family, Peter, John and the redoubtable Lovey. In an old print she is seen crossing the quay at Christchurch, apparently a rather buxom girl, though dainty of face and ankle. She has in fact just come off a ship and is wound tightly about with smuggled lace and silk, under her cloak.

A short distance eastward lies Smugglers Road car-park. From here a sunken way terraces round the hillside back towards Knaves Ash, deep enough to hide a tall man – when the bracken has grown up it would hide a horse and rider. Climbing another path to the top of the ridge, we could look across to Castle Top or southward over a vast heathland which all seemed remote from the coast and the common image of smugglers sneaking up cliff paths from the beach. But once landed the contraband was distributed right through Hampshire, to Wiltshire and beyond. We set out to find the smugglers' market.

Our way lay along the exhilarating ridge walk to Vereley Hill, dog violets the first points of colour along the path, larks springing up from old heather, a far curlew crying. On the summit of Vereley there stood for many years a tower used by the Forestry Commission as a vantage point for fire-watching. Its place has been taken now by a radio mast helping the Commission's keepers and other officials to keep in touch – especially valuable in case of fire.

Long ago it was known as a vantage point. If the Warnes heard that the Revenue men were on the hunt and it was dangerous to move smuggled goods, Lovey would put on her red cloak and stand on Vereley Hill: at night a red lantern was hoisted to the top of the tallest oak. When this tree eventually fell in a storm, the iron ring and staple which held the rope could still be seen rusted into the wood.

Our way led down a holly-covered slope – the forest name for a holly wood is holm – skirting a bog and crossing a stream. A kestrel hovered high above, head down, searching for pippits maybe in the bordering heathland. A bright yellow butterfly, a brimstone, darted down the ride as we entered Ridley Wood, as if to show the way. Huge old oaks and tall beeches stretched away on either side, with here and there small hollies, the oaks in fat bronze buds, the beech capricious, some just showing tender green leaves, some still brown, while here and there a tree stood almost full leafed.

Not so many dead trees as in Mark Ash. In one still standing, a pair of stock doves had nested, flying off at our approach leaving the young to peer down from a hole in the high branch already stripped of bark. The stump of another was entirely covered with star moss, like deep green fur. A grey squirrel scampered across the path, shot up an oak, claws scrabbling on the trunk though not disturbing a missel thrush who sang a song from a topmost branch. Between the massive roots grew little tumps of bun moss, shining silvery green.

The smugglers' road through Ridley crossed ours at right angles, but it would be quite easy to miss it, since the path levels out before intersecting. Presently we turned off to the left and found the deep sunken lane coming up from Picket Post, drifted with dead leaves, mossy banks bound by long, snaking roots of beeches, patched with ivy, a few small hollies, haunt of wren.

Geoffrey Morley, in his book on Hampshire smugglers, suggests that they used it not only as a secret route but as a market place. 'The market held regularly was attended by buyers from all over the Forest, Winchester, Salisbury and even Bristol. It is probable that the finer wares, such as lace from Venice, Bruge, Brussels, brocades from the Middle East and embroideries from all over the world were laid out under the great beeches of Ridley Wood.'

Down a much busier sunken way, the road through Burley Street, we came to Burley itself, clustered round its crossroads in a deep wooded hollow, church, manor and shops all quite close and so appearing deceptively compact – much of Burley is hidden away elsewhere down forest lanes, elegant houses in their own grounds often with pasture for the family horses. Their owners would hardly appreciate John Wise's comment in 1883, 'Burley is one of the most primitive of forest hamlets,' though it is part of Burley's charm that the rest of his description still applies, 'The village suddenly losing itself among the holms and hollies, and then reforming itself again in some open space.'

It grew up round the manor house, a cluster of smallholdings and later servants' cottages. The first Great House was built by Richard de Burley, Bailiff of Burley Bailiwick. In 1251 Richard forfeited the manor to the king, for trespass, but was later granted it back, with an increase in tax. In the next century Sir Simon de Burley was tutor to the Black Prince, but his son, Richard II, had him thrown into the Tower of London for treason and there he was executed, the manor being again forfeit to the king, its tenants unknown until it became the property of the Batten family and then of the Mowbrays.

In 1780 James Mowbray pulled down the old house and built another, Georgian style, laying out the park, in the eighteenth-century fashion, with a lake, lodge and walled garden – some of the great trees date from this time. The Bell Oak held the rope and bell which summoned the estate workers. James left the manor to his sisters, but it was really ruled by their steward, Thomas Eyre. Determined to leave his mark on Burley, he erected stones all round the village. Under Castle Hill one is inscribed 'Rest and be thankful', with his name, another stands opposite the Queen's Head pub. Facing the manor gates another commemorates the short-lived Peace of Paris treaty and reads 'Thomas Eyre, 1802. To Ringwood 5, Christchurch 8.'

However, when Thomas represented the Misses Mowbray at a court hearing, he lost the case, and the Crown regained part of the estate. In 1850 the house was burned down and a new one, in Elizabethan style, built by William Esdaile.

We began our walk round the village at the church, hidden away down a leafy lane. From the hillock of the churchyard we could look across parkland to the manor house among its tall trees; the russet brick gables and tall chimneys made a picturesque 'Tudor' image and must have taken in many a visitor.

New Forest Ponies: Foal in ancient woodland

Mare and foal, Whitefield Moor

New Forest ponies shading, King's Garden

Agister branding New Forest pony

Verderers inspecting stallion for release on forest

New Forest pony sale

The original manor probably had its own chapel: a document dated 1663 mentions 'a tenement called the Chapel' and a field called Chapel Haye, now a housing estate, but Burley was attached to Ringwood parish and had no village church until 1839. The Misses Mowbray had left the manor house to Charles Lefevre MP for Reading: it was his family who gave the land, then called Barn Close, for the site of the church.

The building, which cost £1,000, has a single aisle and though small gives an impression of spaciousness and light. HMS *Burley* presented it with a White Ensign in 1858.

Walking back towards the village, we come to a large pub, the Queen's Head, its brick gabled front disguising what is probably the oldest house in Burley. Inside, it really is everyone's dream of an olde worlde pub, with low ceilings, massive beams, log fires in great brick fireplaces, carved panels, oak chests and hundreds of horse brasses.

Mark Way Bar takes its name from the road across a nearby hill where, tradition tells, coaches were frequently held up by the local highwaymen: Warnes Bar of course commemorates the smuggling family. During recent alterations a hidden cellar was discovered beneath the Stable Bar, pistols, bottles and old coins betraying another smugglers' secret. The Queen's Bar was once the village forge. On the wall hangs a list of publicans: the first was John Youngs in 1699, when the rates were 4d a year.

Across the road, you might well think 'The Witches' Coven' just another 'ye olde' name for a shop out to attract tourists, but in fact it is named after Sybil Leek, who lived in the cottage behind and practised witchcraft, of the white, or good, variety she maintained. However, she dressed like the other kind, in a long black cloak with a crow on her shoulder, which upset many local people. When her lease was not renewed, she went to the United States and made a reputation as a clairvoyant in the 1960s. She was the author of many books on the occult, including *Diary of a Witch.*

The manor grounds lie along one side of the narrow, busy street, cottage shops line the other, selling that curious mixture of genuine antique and cheap twee ornaments supposed all over England to be what visitors want, so that a fine Victorian lustre

Ponies in pound after drift, South Oakley

vase stands between a plaster rabbit and a small plastic witch. It was a relief to find Burley Pottery, where we watched a bowl being thrown on the wheel: after firing, it would be painted subtle shades of brown which distinguish all the jugs, bowls and vases round the walls, no pair of them quite the same.

Outside, a trap goes by, drawn by a beautifully matched pair of ponies, and we are reminded of the real life of Burley which goes on winter and summer. Horsey Burley, you might say. The manor, now Burley Manor Hotel, advertise hunting, tuition and riding – a ride went out as we walked up the long drive.

American troops were stationed here during the last war: the lake was drained and many fine trees disappeared, including the Bell Oak. But now all is peaceful, wide-spaced oaks just springing into leaf above acres of rolling grassland, two chestnut mares grazing, the lake restored. Inside, the conference room has been named after William Esdaile, builder of this house, and indeed his mark is everywhere for like Thomas Eyre he believed in leaving inscriptions in stone. There are Latin mottoes over the fireplace, while his family one is carved over the fine staircase. 'Courage is my protection and glory', it translates.

Along Burley Street, which straggles away into the forest, is an interesting old cottage, cruck built: in the gable end you can see the two crooked or cruck beams forming the framework, stretching from ground level to roof. On the Lyndhurst road stands a Congregational chapel founded (though this is not the original building) by Thomas Eyre. He also endowed a fund to provide twelve poor women with shoes, petticoats and blankets. At Mill Lawn, where the mill once stood, we saw our first foal of the spring just staggering to his feet.

Burley Lodge along the road was once the official house of the Bailiff of the Bailiwick of Burley, seat of the Dukes of Bolton for many years. Though the old house has been replaced, the estate is still famous for the Twelve Apostles, huge old oak trees well spaced beside the drive, said to be six hundred years old, though now only eight Apostles remain. (This is private land.)

The name Burley is said to derive from Saxon words meaning 'the fortified place in the clearing', referring to the castle. From its rampart we could look down on the village and see how, for all its scattered nature, it is still an island in a sea of forest. It was not so long ago that a Burley man's new wife was clouted when she walked down the street – a foreigner she was, came from Brockenhurst ...

Not far from Burley we visited a wild fowl farm, in a delightful situation, a series of ponds and little lakes terracing down a gentle green slope protected on three sides by deep woodlands. In the first spacious pens strutted brilliant pheasants with their sober wives, a golden pheasant, another with red breast and a gold cowl and, brightest of all, Reeves with blue and green wings and a red rump: in the pale sunshine a monal pheasant from the Himalayas shone all the colours of a peacock.

Below this paddock the birds roamed free, though with clipped wings. Alders and willows in first yellow-green leaf leaned over banks bright with daffodils, and clear water slipped past in streams and ponds, always moving and fresh, a landscape natural as grass, it seems, yet all created from a bare slope over the last sixteen years from artesian springs at the top of the rise.

A standing army of barnacle geese, white fronts and South American ashy-headed geese lower their long necks, hiss with menace and finally decide we are not worth attacking. Brown eider duck come waddling up, making little gossipy noises, hoping for a treat of poultry pellets.

The lowest lake has an island in the middle with nest boxes set under the trees, though the eggs of first clutches are taken away to incubators. Ducks paddled about or slept, beak under wing, among hooded mergansers, golden eyes, ruddy ducks from North America and a swallow swooping down for a drink. The most expensive bird of all is the showy red-breasted goose; a pair of ornamental fowl could cost several hundred pounds so it is essential to keep predators at bay. Stoats, hawks and owls can be kept under reasonable control – the most dreaded are mink, escaped from forest mink farms, not only vicious but aquatic and so able to reach the islands. Even so, the farm breeds all its own stock and sells some three thousand birds in a year, not only in Britain but all over Europe and as far away as Canada and Malawi.

Birds fly *in* too. We watched a pair of willow warblers flitting through the reeds. Other visitors over the years have included kingfishers, hobbies and such rarities as golden orioles, osprey and little bustard.

Small rust-coloured ducks, ducks with blue beaks, ducks apparently wearing powder-puffs as hats – there seemed an endless variety in this sheltered green world; in fact a hundred species live here altogether. The farm is not open to casual visitors, only to those intending to buy, a commercial venture new to the forest but flourishing in its secluded corner.

Coming south from Burley under a grey sky, the heathland rolls away on either hand, dark and wild, mantled in old heather, threatening as Hardy's Egdon. Brushing through tough bushes of ling three feet high, we startled a lark into the air and three rabbits into their burrows. On the bare earth of their warren an adder lay coiled, a darkish brown zigzagged with black. Sensing our approach, probably through the ground vibrating since its sight and hearing are poor, it slithered unhurriedly away.

Today we look upon the word 'viper' as a rather old-fashioned alternative name for adder, but the old foresters maintain it is a separate species, smaller, ruddy in colour and more vicious. This cannot be a confusion with the New Forest's own variety, the smooth snake, for that is grey. We had arranged to meet Dickie and hear more about vipers.

The heathland road led onto Thorney Hill, a scatter of dwellings some of them built to re-house the gypsies who used to camp here, then along the fringe of the forest, invaded now by farmland, to Wootton, a hamlet set among flat commons and tamed pastures, a farm hidden in trees, bungalows, nothing very old it would seem, yet the name Wootton goes back many centuries, variously spelt Wodeton, Wodynton, Woditune. It occurs in a forest survey of 1291. 'A messuage, orchard and courtyard of Batrameslye and Wodinton which was Eustace Fuchir's worth by the year 13/4; one hundred and twelve acres of land worth 4d an acre, 37/4; meadow, moor, a grove and pasture worth 6/4; fixed rent for the year 71/2½; two pounds of pepper worth 8d a pound; customary pannage 6d; service and work for the year 12 shillings; cocks and hens for church-scot [a tax] 10/-. From which Jennifer who was the wife of Eustace has recovered a third part as a dowry.'

When the railway came, Marsdens, the brewers of Poole, built five pubs to cash in on the new trade, though it was a two-day job delivering the beer to them by wagon and horses. One of these pubs was the Rising Sun, which has picnic tables on pleasant lawns. To appreciate its special feature though, you must go inside and look out. All the windows and the door are patterned with stained glass in Art Deco designs. The windows glow with formalized tulips in orange, yellow and green, while the door panel is of course that favourite motif, the rising sun, recently redesigned and beautifully restored.

Here we met Dickie and asked him if he'd seen an adder yet.

'Ah, you get plenty o'they round yer,' he said. 'My nipper used to catch 'em and send 'em up to the zoo in London. There's all kinds of adder you know. The black and white, he've got a sort o'yellow orangy colour round the mouth – that's the male. They females now is all sorts 'colours. You can have the chestnut, the liver chestnut, the black and yellow, then there's the real black – they'm very rare. Just like black velvet they looks.'

We asked him to describe the ones he called vipers.

'They ain't very big, they red'uns, nine to ten inches is about the limit. You don't see many of them about, anyhow, but they'll spring at you, high enough to git yer hand.'

Dickie had spent all his life in the forest, could remember when parts of it were impenetrable woods and swamps in the 1920s before the Forestry Commission began to lay down the network of tracks now taken for granted, so we listened with respect to his views. However, zoologists tell us firmly that there is only one species of adder in Britain. So are these small red jumping 'vipers' really the active young ones?

Turning northward back into forest proper, we passed the tall beeches and conifers of Wilverley, the young beech leaves brilliant against dark pines, and came to a vast flat expanse of grassland, gorse and old bracken called Wilverley Plain, famous for the Naked Man, rearing up in its midst.

This is the remains of an oak tree said to have been used as a gibbet. On a map of 1789 it bears that name and so presumably was dead then. For many years it held up two great bare arms to the sky and was shored up by struts, but even so eventually fell and now the base is set in concrete. Today, inside a small wooden enclosure the Naked Man stands only ten feet high, with one pale, barkless arm flung out. Tradition has it that John King, the last highwayman to threaten travellers on Markway Hill, was hanged from a branch of the Naked Man, though later we were to hear another version.

Walking in the northern forest one day, near Bramshaw, we met with Wilfred, who passed on to us this version of the folklore surrounding the Naked Man.

Mark Way, an impressionable young man, was witness to a hold-up by a highwayman called Picket who got away with a rich haul. Deciding this was an easy way to get rich, Mark too became a highwayman, eventually acquiring so much jewellery he needed to sell it. So he and Picket set out for Winchester but were apprehended, Picket being shot. Mark Way was injured by shot also, but this did not prevent his being hanged, from a convenient oak tree. That night a great storm broke over Wilverley, and the body was struck by lightning which ripped off its clothes, leaving, of course, a naked man …

Wilfred said he had read all this in an old book which had been found hidden beneath the wall of a house at Sway, which was being repaired – it had once been a blacksmith's shop.

Whatever the truth, the name Markway has been used again in this century. The New Forest Act of 1949 allowed the inclosure of up to a further five thousand acres, with the consent of the Verderers. It was decided that these new inclosures should be sited where deer and ponies were most frequently killed by traffic. North of Wilverley Plain stands one such new inclosure, doubly fenced from the road with a band of improved grazing between the fences and access solely back into the forest. This is called Markway Inclosure and must have saved scores of animal lives.

How better to end the day than with tea at the station? Holmsley Station was originally called Christchurch Road, since opposition from landowners prevented the line going on to the south coast as originally planned. Several of the cottages round about were once stables for the carriage traffic: passengers were picked up at Christchurch Road and taken on tc Christchurch or Bournemouth. Eventually the line was extended to Ringwood. When it was closed down, stretches of it were taken over as roads, and the old station house has now become a restaurant. Park your car on the old platform overlooking a particularly straight stretch of line/road and you can have tea in the station yard, now lawns with a view over the peaceful green acres of Holmsley Bog.

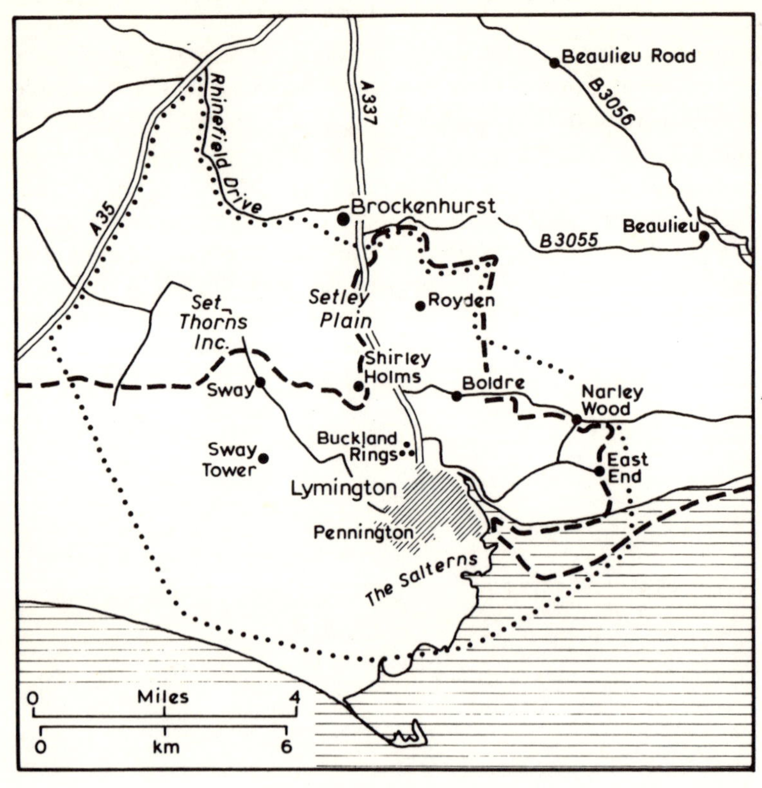

Around Lymington

3 *Around Lymington*

Following the line of old railway eastward towards Lymington, we come to Setthorns Inclosure, a deceptive wood presenting a long, straight frontage to the road of dark, forbidding pines. But once inside, the wood is revealed as a whole collection of little copses, a stand of oak here, a sweet chestnut there, with groves of birch and ash spread about and open glades between of bracken and bramble, a few late bluebells – and all threaded with winding gravel tracks, for this is a Forestry Commission camping site.

Since camping on the open forest was forbidden, the Commission have developed three grades of site: Class A, such as the enormous site at Holmsley where there is room for seven hundred units and every facility laid on; Class B, called semi-equipped, and Class C, informal, to which Setthorns belongs. This site offers running water and waste-disposal, camping gas and telephone available, spaces for light tents and information to be found at the camp office, but bring your own loo. Each caravan has its own clearing in the woods with gravel hard standing. Some had thrown out a tented wing, giving a glimpse of dining-table and chairs, all very civilized among the blackbirds and great tits. Here was the old railway line again, now running through a sheltered gorge overhung with birch and willows in woolly catkin, site for several trailers but doubling as a footpath stretching enticingly away into a green distance.

Three boys were playing Tarzan on long ropes slung from the trees; dogs are not allowed in all camps but may visit Setthorns, and several new arrivals were casing their new home ground, while a missel thrush sang overhead, beak into the wind – it can hold 270 caravans and tents yet still feel spacious and uncrowded.

Most sites open mid-April and close at the end of September. Setthorns is the only one in the whole forest to stay open all the year round, sheltered from cold winds on its southerly slope.

From Setthorns we come to Sway on the forest edge, a village which began life as three manors, Sway Quarr, Sway Romsey and Sway Christchurch. After the commons were enclosed, it became a farming place with many smallholdings, but even today, with the railway come and gone and a church of its own, it lacks a centre, still straggles round a maze of lanes.

One name will be familiar to all brought up on Captain Marryat's *The Children of the New Forest* – Arnewood. Spelled without the 'e', this is the name of the Royalist mansion burned by the Roundheads from which old Jacob rescued the four children: it was just south of the forest near Lymington. Though the book is fiction, it throws an interesting light on the Civil War period. Jacob was a Verderer, appointed and paid by the King. With King Charles no longer in power, he received no wages but felt entitled to live off the forest, eating and selling venison, till Parliament appointed their own intendent who demanded to know how the Verderers have lived without payment!

Jacob had to go into Lymington to buy salt for preserving meat through the winter, reminding us that Lymington was the salt capital of the south of England.

The other feature of Sway known to many who have never visited the village, is the tower, visible from the Isle of Wight – island children were told it was called Sway Tower because it swayed in a high wind! However familiar it may be as a finger on the skyline, close to, it rears to a majestic height, dwarfing the houses beneath.

Andrew Peterson was born in Yorkshire in 1803. After studying law, he went to India where he became fascinated by the potential of concrete, then a new building material. When he retired, he returned to England and settled at Sway, buying a house at Arnewood, where he experimented with concrete, putting up various outhouses and a small tower.

He became concerned at the number of local men who were unemployed. Having become interested in the realm of spiritualism, he sought guidance there as to how he could bring work to the neighbourhood and told friends that he had received instructions from the spirit of Sir Christopher Wren (architect of St Paul's Cathedral) that he should take on workmen and build a great tower – of concrete, naturally.

Begun in 1879, it took six years to build, the buckets of liquid concrete being drawn up on a pulley worked at ground level by a horse. Today, the lower half is a private house, while the upper, with its tall windows still unglazed, is home to countless pigeons and jackdaws.

Sway Tower has stood for a hundred years now, vindicating all its designer's theories about the new building material, but one has to say it has not weathered kindly, only darkened to brownish grey, whereas stone would have gained the subtle shadings of moss and lichen.

However, our next call on the way to Lymington bore shades of every conceivable hue. Forest Crafts began as a small venture in a stable at Burley, in 1960: now it sprawls all over the ancient farmhouse of Yaldhurst at Pennington, set among wide lawns and mature trees.

Inside, every room is overflowing with handicrafts, all of them made in the New Forest or close by, the work of some five hundred exhibitors. The nursery was piled with brilliant-coloured stuffed toys, from a tiny ladybird to a life-size pierrot dancer: other rooms showed hats, shawls and jackets made from handspun wool, and hand-woven skirts. Watercolours, marmalade, cushions, walking-sticks – there seemed no end to the variety.

We were looking especially for crafts relating directly to the forest. One table held glass delicately engraved with squirrel, pony and kingfishers, another showed stationery hand-printed with fallow deer designs. Forest wood provided the raw material for garden tools, bowls of all sizes and a finely carved otter. Ponies figured on pottery, and a copper panel: everywhere along the walls hung forest scenes, from a bold panorama of tawny trees, autumn at Bolderwood, to a detailed drawing of twisty beech roots.

Often visitors can watch craftsmen at work, making pottery for example, or spinning. In the evenings there are classes going on: at the moment you can take a course in oil painting, wood turning or weaving, carrying on the tradition of forest crafts.

Across the sandy stretch of Pennington Common we made for the very oldest part of Lymington, a town outside the New Forest bounds but, like Ringwood, intimately connected with it down the years through shipbuilding, the salt trade, the highway of Lymington River and of course the weekly market.

Buckland Manor, a fifteenth-century farmhouse, is now a hotel with sunken garden, the promise of log fires and free-range eggs; Buckland Vineyard revives a Roman skill, but oldest of all is Buckland Rings, an Iron Age fort, seven acres enclosed in great ramparts and ditches above the river valley.

Below it, on the river itself, where the Passford Brook flows in, there stood an ancient dock called Ampress, strategically placed at the last reach of the tide up the estuary (before the embankment was built), its six acres now lost beneath a factory.

Buckland lacks some of its perimeter banks – it is a rectangle really, with rounded corners, never a ring – but the remains are still impressive. Some land was levelled for agriculture in the eighteenth century, and the flat centre is now pastureland, and private, but a public footpath leads along the northern boundary. To anyone used to the windswept heights of Grimspound or Maiden Castle, the site is a surprise. True, Buckland stands on a natural hillock, but this end of it is covered with woodland, on a May morning full of birdsong and moving leaf shadows.

Below the lane, the brook wanders through Sheepwash Bottom, past a grove of cherry all in blossom, silvery birches and clumps of kingcups shining gold in the sun. A chiff-chaff calls over and over. Beside the path grow ferns, ferny-leaved wood anemones and delicate pale pink flowers of wood sorrel, while on our right the wood rises dramatically to the beech-crowned northern rampart of Buckland Rings. This delightful path brought us abruptly to the roaring A337 to Brockenhurst: what a pity more of the Rings cannot be explored. (The interesting-looking banks at the eastern end are merely the remains of an old sand pit.)

When Buckland was excavated, the banks were found to be strengthened with turf courses and a small amount of limestone brought up from the beach. The very few artefacts discovered dated it Iron Age: in all its seven acres only one hearth was found, presumably the floor of a hut, so perhaps these huge ditches and banks were built against an invasion which never happened.

Toward Lymington on the corner of Hollywood Lane a high, curved brick wall all but hides the mellow tiles of Buckland Cottage, home for many years of Caroline Bowles, a local poet whom we shall meet again at Boldre.

Lymington's splendidly wide High Street slopes down between Georgian houses, shop fronted, to the river, but it was not always so spacious – an earlier town hall reared on pillars jutted right out across the street, and down its centre once stood rows of permanent market stalls. Old prints show the church mantled in ivy. This is stripped clean now, and a new parish hall built onto the church on the north side.

Inside, the oldest stones date back to the founding of a chapel here, subordinate to Boldre, for hundreds of years the parish church. During the Civil War it was occupied by Cromwell's soldiers and badly damaged, but renovated after the Restoration of Charles II when the tower was built. Today the galleries lend it an eighteenth-century air. The dominating east window in shades of blues and greys tends to make that end rather gloomy, but its subject, of Christ stilling the storm, with the text 'They that go down to the sea in ships', is splendidly appropriate to Lymington.

Many memorials on the walls bear the name Burrard, celebrating the family who provided Members of Parliament for Lymington for many years until the Reform Act – it was a Burrard who built a town hall in 1710.

On the north wall of the old mortuary chapel are two delightful modern stained-glass windows. One shows a family – a boy with a racquet, a girl with her hand on the dog's head; behind mother, father and the baby, a narrow lane winds away into the distance.

Outside, traffic roars up and down the street, but we turned aside for a moment into the churchyard. In contrast, here all is peace, wide stretches of grass and gravestones intersected by little paths leading off to playing-fields and avenues of old limes.

Crossing the traffic and passing Monmouth House, one of the many elegant Georgian buildings, we turned into Church Lane, narrow and quiet, hung with old trees. Elm Grove House has a wonderful wall, curving in and out, in and out – the proper name is serpentine. Ivy-leaned toadflax and small bellflowers grow among its mellow bricks. Further along on the opposite side there is a modern example, but the curves seem too sharply angled and already parts of it lean. It was built by Dennis Wheatley, writer of many famous thrillers, including *The Haunting of Toby Jug*, when he lived at Grove Place, now pulled down. In fact, this part of Lymington has many old brick walls, some of them forming a network of little alleyways connecting with courtyards leading into High Street.

As we turned into All Saints Road, pleasantly shaded with tall trees, a grey squirrel swung across over our heads from oak to sycamore, shot into a hole and turned round to scold us, a reminder that the forest is never far away.

Rookes Lane brought us to Woodside Gardens, once the site of the Rooke family mansion: though the house has gone, many trees remain from the original garden, notably a huge monkey puzzle and tall, tawny-barked Wellingtonias. Here stands the horse trough from the top of the High Street, now full of polyanthus, and also five pillars from the old town hall – five more lie prone on the grass.

Wooded lanes bring us to a pub once the heart of the enormous Lymington salt industry – the Chequers. The name is said to be a pun, for this was headquarters of the Salt Duty Collectors, who checked weight against tax.

Maiden Dock is a narrow channel running up through the marshes to Creek Cottage. Boats used to bring coal up to the jetty here, discharge it and take on cargoes of salt. On a breezy May morning gulls called from the marsh, swallows skimmed the water and a scent of wallflowers filled the air – these grew out of two picturesque old brick buildings with undulating roof lines and massive buttresses which remain from the salt-drying days.

Salt-making began here before the twelfth century. Shallow, flat-bottomed pits or pans were dug out of the marshes and allowed to flood with sea water: when the sun had partially evaporated it, the solution was drawn off into boiling-houses, where salt was crystallized out in big copper vessels heated latterly by coal fires. When the industry was at its height in the early eighteenth century, there were 163 pans in the Lymington area: windmills were used to help pump up the brine. In 1784 Thomas Rowlandson, the artist, came to Hampshire on a sketching tour: the fruits of this include vivid drawings of workers in the boiling-house, and also of the wind pumps.

For hundreds of years the New Forest commoners came into Lymington to buy salt, their only means of preserving meat. Four thousand tons a year were sold on average at the beginning of the nineteenth century, but then a slow decline set in, hastened by the very high tax on salt occasioned by the Napoleonic Wars, the cost of coal and finally the discovery of mineral salt in Cheshire, easily distributed by the growing network of railways. So by about 1870 the salt pans were gradually falling into disuse. Some were taken over to breed oysters, others drained and filled in to provide more pasture land. Recently some have been turned into a sheltered lake where children can safely learn to sail.

From Creek Cottage, footpaths led off in all directions, one of them the long-distance Solent Path with its distinctive blue seagull flash, but we chose to wander out along the bank of Maiden Creek into a vast, flat green world beneath a blue sky eddying with white wings and the crying of gulls, glimpses of the far sea, creeks shining here and there and the far downs of the Isle of Wight our southern horizon – miles from anywhere, it seemed, all remote and peaceful, yet just to the east a forest of masts betrayed the vast marina in Lymington River.

On our right, Friesians grazed the old salt pans, now sweet grass, though many dikes and ditches remain. Suddenly from the ditch beside us a cormorant sprang into the air, so close we could see the white cheek patch and strange green eye. Where the creek widened out, a fan of sandy beach made a perfect bird-watching place from which we could see curlew probing the mudflats opposite with their long, curved beaks, a redshank, his legs shining bright orange, and dunlin scuttling about like clockwork toys among the larger turnstones.

In winter the population changes, with rafts of duck and flocks of Brent geese; grazing – even an osprey may pass by, but today larks sang above a dike golden with gorse bloom, and far out, gulls clamoured over the sea – the salterns make an exhilarating walk at any time of year.

A path along their landward edge leads to Kings Saltern Road and the riverside, where there are lawns and seats from which to watch the water traffic and admire the hundreds of yachts in the Haven or the swans tranquilly ignoring them all. Here too are the boatyards which in their ancient beginnings were a direct link with the forest. Edward I ordered Lymington to supply three ships for the Navy but was told, 'The larger ships are at sea in the keeping of God. Only little cogges are left.' By Edward III's reign, Lymington sent nine ships for the Navy, when Portsmouth could supply only five! The town's medieval seal bears a ship.

John Combes owned a shipyard here in 1668. In the next century it was building merchant ships. In 1821 Thomas Inman moved there from Sussex, establishing a famous line of yachts including *Lulworth* and *Alarm*, which raced America round the Isle of Wight in 1851, a forerunner of the America Cup series. This in turn has become the large and busy Berthon Boatyard.

One merchantman needed an incredible number of timber loads, mostly oak but some beech and elm, because so much went to waste. Very tall, thin trunks were needed for masts, tall, thick ones to be sawn up for planking, but most wastage occurred with trees which had to yield a particular shaped timber, such as a stern post which had to be a shallow V. By 1800 there was great concern that the forest had been so stripped of mature trees. The New Forest Enclosure Act was passed to ensure new supplies – fortunately never felled, as iron-clad ships took over: some of the splendid old oaks in the forest date from this planting.

Discovering the New Forest: Riding school

Angels Farm Pottery

The Dark Shepherd by
Greta Hopkinson

Shirley Holms Activity Farm

Holmsley Wild Fowl Reserve

Canadian Memorial, Mogshade

Blackwater Picnic Site, Rhinefield

Caravans at Long Beech

Yachtsmen's cottages, all brightly painted, and boatyards lead us to the Quay, the Isle of Wight ferryboat looming enormous among all the small craft.

William Allingham, the Victorian poet, was Customs officer for Lymington from 1863, his office a small room above the Coastguard Station. Depressed at leaving London, he was nevertheless able to write in his diary, 'I felt a great deliciousness in the quiet green lanes and hedges, thickets, woods and distances and in the evening after my arrival, at the field gate close to the town I heard four nightingales.' Through friendship with the Cloughs, and Julia Cameron, the pioneer photographer at Freshwater on the Isle of Wight, he achieved a cherished ambition to be introduced to Tennyson. After being entertained at Farringford, he became an ardent disciple. 'From Custom House window see Tennyson on board steamer as she passes and hurry to station,' says his diary.

The Old Customs House on Quay Hill is now a picture gallery specializing in nineteenth-century marine and landscape paintings.

Picturesque Quay Hill with its cobbles and elegant bow-windowed boutiques brings us back to the High Street, sloping up between modern shop fronts, but raise your eyes above them and most of the houses are revealed as Georgian, with crooked roofscapes or some unusual carving – there are still some fine Georgian buildings untouched, but most of them are away from the shopping centre.

This broad main street was the site for the May Fair, the charter for which was granted in 1257, when forest commoners would bring in their cattle and horses to sell, as well as their produce of cheese, leather and honey. A Victorian fair is described in William Allingham's diary, rather disapprovingly: 'Booths in the streets with toys and sweets, noise and clatter. Shows – some monkeys and a wild boar. Dancing booth – shooting galleries. Gypsies, black eyed girls in tawdry bright attire and brown old witches.' Not the kind of people you met at Farringford ... but an occasion when folk would have journeyed into Lymington from all over the forest.

Just as they flock in today to the Saturday market! Come

early to see what is on the stalls lining both sides of the street, for by midday it is often difficult to move from one to another for the press of customers and lookers-on. The atmosphere is less homely than Ringwood: there are no little auctions going on in corners and no livestock, but the variety of stalls is amazing, from fresh vegetables, meat and fish to all kinds of clothes, tools, brassware, health foods and second-hand saucepans.

We can cross the river by walking over the bridge or catching a train from the town station to the harbour; there are plans for turning the upper storey of the Victorian, brick station house into a museum for Lymington.

We walked, on our right the wide harbour, a few rowing boats at moorings, further down the yacht haven masts and the Isle of Wight ferry terminal, ahead the land rises and on its wooded summit a tall stone finger points to the sky. On our left the river narrows, quiet and unvisited, winding up to Boldre through banks of reeds still cut annually for thatching, home for birds such as Cetti's warbler.

Much of the land ahead belonged to the Walhampton estate, home of the Burrard family for many years, now a school. Admiral Sir Harry Burrard Neale, MP for forty years, entertained George III at Walhampton and was a pall-bearer at the funeral of William IV: when he died, in 1840, the dowager Queen Adelaide and others had this granite obelisk raised in his memory on the highest point of the estate. There used to be a panoramic view of Lymington from its steps, but trees have grown up now to obscure it: last time we visited the obelisk, the south side was strewn with owl pellets – the grey fur and minute bones of fieldmice.

Another minor Victorian poet, Coventry Patmore, lived here by the harbour. He moved from Hastings to 'The Lodge', now Ferry Point House, in 1891. In these last years of his life he was largely occupied in editing his essays rather than writing poetry – perhaps the domestic burden was too heavy. The Lodge had eight sitting-rooms and stood in four acres of grounds. He wrote in his diary, 'I dream of owning a disused railway carriage in the heart of the forest, cutting all ties and living alone. There would be two compartments, one for night and one for day.'

Boldre is not in the heart of the forest, but he could have tucked his railway carriage away there in green seclusion: more of an area than a village, its narrow leafy lanes meander along the river, sometimes crossing it by ford or narrow bridge, passing secluded houses hidden behind high walls or many trees – that afford only a glimpse of azalea beds, mown lawns – it was not always so civilized.

William Gilpin, head of Cheam School for twenty-five years, retired in 1777 and was offered the living of Boldre by an old pupil, whose father, William Mitford, had built Exbury House, near Beaulieu. On taking up residence, the Rev. Gilpin found 'the lower class of parishioner were little better than a gang of gypsies – utterly neglected by former pastors, exposed to every temptation of pillage and robbery.' A man of immense energy, he built a school first. The boys were taught reading, writing and the first four rules of arithmetic, the girls to read, knit and spin, and to sew and mend their own clothes. The master was paid £24 a year, the mistress £12.

Boldre was a vast parish at this time, including the whole of Lymington: besides caring for it, William Gilpin was writing *Forest Scenary* and making a large number of drawings of the countryside which he later sold to provide an endowment for the school.

The building called Gilpin's Cottage now is still there on the corner of School Lane, though dormers have been added on. Opposite to it, Gilpin built a poorhouse. This was eventually pulled down and the new school built on its site – the memorial tablet on the original school has been transferred to it.

The first mayflowers showed white in high hedges, scenting the air, while campion and stitchwort showed red and white on the lower banks. With good boots it is possible to walk up the river bank to Boldre, from near Lymington, the way Caroline Bowles must have come, for she describes it exactly in her poem 'The Evening Walk':

My lonely ramble yester-eve I took,
Along the pleasant path that by the brook
Skirting its flowery margin, winds away

Through fields all fragrant now with new mown hay,
Gathering the wild flowers on that streamlet's edge,
Spared by the mower's scythe, a fringing ledge
Of golden crowsfoot, waving meadowsweet,
And wilding rose, that dipped the stream to meet.

Caroline Bowles lived across the stream in the house we passed under Buckland Rings. Here she grew up a freckled, outdoor tomboy, climbing trees, riding her pony and caring for a menagerie of rescued pets, a wounded leveret, a one-legged bullfinch, a trapped squirrel and motherless lambs. As a girl she met Robert Southey and Wordsworth – later she was to write a long autobiographical poem called 'The Birthday', perhaps modelled on Wordsworth's 'Prelude', in which there is a description of a visit to William Gilpin at Boldre. Amid her pets at Buckland Cottage, birds, rabbits, spaniels, a toad, a grey parrot, she wrote to Robert Southey, and their correspondence continued for nineteen years. After his wife died, Southey married her and went to live at the cottage, where 'he could be seen hard at work near the window of one of the upper rooms, a small panelled apartment, scarcely big enough for a really comfortable study'.

Caroline Bowles Southey's collected poems and a book called *Chapters on Country Churchyards* are full of pleasant and perceptive descriptions of Boldre and the forest country close by.

William Bromfield did not live to catalogue the flowers on Boldre's banks. His family moved to the Isle of Wight where he became passionately interested in its wild flowers, studying every species to be found at first hand, in between botanical trips to the West Indies and North America. Having almost finished his island study, he determined to enlarge its scope, to take in Hampshire, including the New Forest, but before this could be set in hand he was tempted to take one more journey, this time to the Near East. He died of fever in Damascus aged a mere forty-nine. When his *Flora Vectensis* was posthumously published, it ran to some 670 pages and still makes fascinating reading.

If the houses are hidden from each other among these gentle, winding lanes, Boldre church is far from them all, on a green knoll above the river, with wide views westward across the woods and pastures of the valley to the forest beyond. The churchyard is ringed by big old trees – including a field maple, the brightest of greens in spring – which soften the outline of a fortress-like tower dating from the fourteenth century. Here, beneath the remains of another maple, William Gilpin lies buried. It was not only the parishioners he had found wanting, but the building too, for he wrote in a letter of 1787, 'Some time ago I was engaged in the same business with my church – that is to make it decent. I made a neat cornice – gave capitals of my pillars – tinted the whole a light leaden colour and turned a very ugly thing into a very decent parish church.'

He also wrote the epitaph which appears on his table tomb. 'In a quiet mansion beneath this stone, secured from the affliction and the still more dangerous enjoyments of life, lie the remains of William Gilpin.'

On the church wall stands a memorial to William Bromfield, and here Caroline Bowles was married to Robert Southey.

Today it is rather more than decent – a beautiful light interior under a waggon roof ornamented with brightly painted bosses. Though much restored, its oldest stones include Norman arches, and the church is full of treasures from every age, a breeches Bible, thirteenth-century porch, smiling carved heads, a memorial painting of HMS *Hood* and a wealth of colourful needlework all provided by the church's own guild.

The east window too shimmers with colour, violet, crimson and canary where Christ reigns in glory from the cross, the Holy Spirit hovering above in semi-abstract design – a most striking feature, given in 1967. Boldre church is a heartening place, for many of its windows, the lectern, curtains and even some of the communion plate have all been given recently, while decaying parts such as the sundial and the roof bosses have been restored by the craftsmanship of Boldre people.

Outside, stitchwort and speedwell tangle in the banks, and we went in search of larger flowers, to Spinners Garden, the drive winding downhill between banks of pink and white camellias, magnolias holding up their waxy flowers all pale against dark shining foliage with blue anemones in drifts beneath, little green spurges, dark cypress; a circular route passes rock-garden banks, tiny pasque flowers, greenhouses and Christmas trees, the discovery of little half-hidden glades making the garden seem larger than it is.

Until 1966 this was forest. The family had a holiday home here, coming for holidays from Malvern: they began to clear a bit of garden ... first the front, then round the side. Now Spinners can be visited all the year round; for a small payment one can enjoy a stroll round its sheltered paths, but its chief role is as supplier of rare plants. These are sent all over Britain, to Japan, America, New Zealand and Europe. One sixth of all the plants are sent abroad.

Spinners specializes in shrubs and plants, particularly ground cover, for the small garden, with particular emphasis on interesting foliage, silver, purple or variegated, and rarities. Because many of the plants are delicate or choosy, the catalogue is not just a list, many species have helpful notes, so the first entry reads, 'Abutilon megapotamicum, pendulous flowers with red calyx and yellow petals last from June till the frost.' The owners are always happy to give advice on what will suit your garden. Not the kind of nursery that offers ordinary herbaceous plants such as lupins and Michaelmas daisies, but a place to find such gems as chequered fritillary, white-flowered kingcup for the bog garden, or green hellbore.

From Spinners we went back into the wilds in search of roe deer to photograph. Brockenhurst Woods Nature Reserve reaches south to Boldre, which here gives its name to a stretch of the river. Waymarked tracks wander through mixed woodlands, groves of birches, their tiny new leaves a haze of green, ancient beeches and old sycamores with bluebells spreading a carpet beneath and a few late primroses. Serious naturalists may obtain permits to study off the paths but we were content to follow the yellow arrows, listening to the songs of the blackcap, nuthatch, glimpsing a tree creeper, a long-tailed tit. From a clearing we heard a high mewing like aerial kittens, and there soaring on blunt wings far above was a pair of buzzards.

Northward the path comes out into a vast, spreading parkland belonging to Brockenhurst Manor, but we turned down towards the river to find 'the house by the Boldre' where the naturalist W.H. Hudson lived while writing *Hampshire Days*, in fact Royden Manor. Across a pasture where black beasts grazed we could see its gable of old rust brick, and urns on a high wall, below which rough grass sloped down to woods hiding the river.

Hudson was born near Buenos Aires in 1841. Instead of going to school he roamed the countryside, becoming a keen naturalist even as a boy – years described in *Far Away and Long Ago*. As a young man he came to England and after many setbacks gradually became known as a writer. When about sixty he came to Royden, falling in love with the New Forest as a 'place of refreshment for body and soul'. The first chapter of *Hampshire Days* is called 'The House on the Boldre'. 'A small, old, picturesque red brick house with high pitched roof and tall chimneys, a great part of it over run with ivy and creepers, the walls and roof stained by time and many coloured lichen to a richly variegated greyish red – the date is cut on stone inside, 1692.'

Here among the half-ruinous outhouses he watched swallows and flycatchers, wagtails and finches, and saw the strange contest between a hornet and a bank vole for a trickle of sweet sap, and the gold-crested wren. 'When the minute bird was sitting on her eggs in her little cradle nest, I would pull down the branch but the little fairy bird refused to quit.' Hudson tended to love birds more than people. He accused the New Forest dwellers of being parasites on the land and held that their habit of cutting so much wood, peat and gorse accounted for such vast stretches of barren heath!

The lane led us down to a wooden footbridge over the Boldre. Looking down into the clear brown water, we could see what appeared to be thousands of tiny fish milling about in a pool, perhaps trout fry, though a fisherman on the bank had had no luck with the adult variety. Oaks hung out over the river, and blackthorn still showed white blossom. In marshy grass bright yellow kingcups grew, roots in water, with pale lilac lady's smock higher up. A grey wagtail landed on a midstream rock, flicked his tail, yellow breast reflected below, and a willow warbler sang out, fittingly from the willows; an adder basked in the sun, and orange-tip butterflies flittered down the sunny aisle of the wood – a day W.H. Hudson would have loved. Only roe deer were missing.

After the peace of Royden Woods it was time for activity – Shirley Holms Activity Farm where the list of things to do takes your breath away before you even set foot to stirrup. This enterprise began some twenty years ago at Passford; now the heart of it is a rambling white house surrounded by stables and yards, beyond them by meadows stretching away to the forest.

All kinds of riding holidays are on offer, from bring-your-own-horse with full board for you both with the opportunity to learn carriage-driving or use the indoor riding-school, to Eager Beaver courses for teenagers, sleeping in a dormitory and earning their rides by helping in the stables. There are Western holidays too, in full gear. Shirley Holms particularly welcomes deprived children from inner city areas: a visit to these 150 green acres can change their lives.

And it is not all horse; there is a swimming-pool, sauna, tennis, all kinds of indoor games, house parties and discos, for the thirty-five residents. This delightful mix brings adults too: show jumpers come year after year from Europe, America, even Japan.

Keeping fifty horses is expensive, even if you let out some of the stables to boarders, and when the slump began several years ago, fewer people could afford riding. So Shirley Holms began a new venture, building up a collection of rare breeds of domestic animals in conjunction with the Rare Breeds Society.

We were taken on a tour of the animals. There was a Berkshire sow, orange with black markings, and a Gloucester spot cross with eleven spotted piglets, little black and white Bagot goats, the billy with proud, back-swept horns, and Vietnamese pot bellies with flat noses, pigs as ugly as their name. Out in the meadows roamed long-horned Highland cattle, a belted Galloway bull, Przewalski ponies with upstanding manes like stiff brushes and extraordinary stumpy-legged little cows called Dexters giving such a high milk yield their udders almost touch the grass. This is important because Shirley Holms aims to be largely self-sufficient, producing its own milk and butter, pork and beef, and wool from Soay, Black Welsh and Jacob sheep which is sheared, spun and woven on the premises. A whole shed full of rabbits makes a paradise for children, but the rabbits are being bred for the table as well. Some animals are just for fun though, like Spencer the llama who spits when annoyed, the raccoon, and Toast and Marmalade the Shetland ponies. We also watched butter being made in the traditional way; other crafts on show are leather tooling, with the wheelwrights and the blacksmith at work.

Not far from Shirley Holms lies another centre for recreation, though this time more limited. Setley Pond is an old gravel pit, now flooded. The Forestry Commission in their cunning way have contrived a car-park right by the water's edge but invisible from the road. The surroundings are still rather gravelly and bleak, but ducks gather on the pond and children splash on the edge. However, Setley is special in one way, rented by the Solent Model Yacht Club. Here every Sunday and Tuesday, enthusiasts can gather and race or manoeuvre their small craft by radio controls.

Setley Plain is a sprawl of heathland handy to Lymington for picnics: elsewhere on its edge is an unpublicized chain of old gravel workings. Here the banks have greened over, making little lawns between the ponds fringed with willows and the air full of fluff drifting from their catkins. Never mind traffic roaring along close by, though invisible, a stonechat was singing from an alder, and bugle made a drift of deep blue beside a muddy patch where ponies came down to drink. Marsh St John's wort grew along wet ledges. There out in clear water was the plant we had come to seek, water violet, raising spires of palest lilac above the surface, each flower of each whorl with a silky yellow centre, a lovely sight, and for the botanist worth two stars in *Collins' Guide to Wildflowers*.

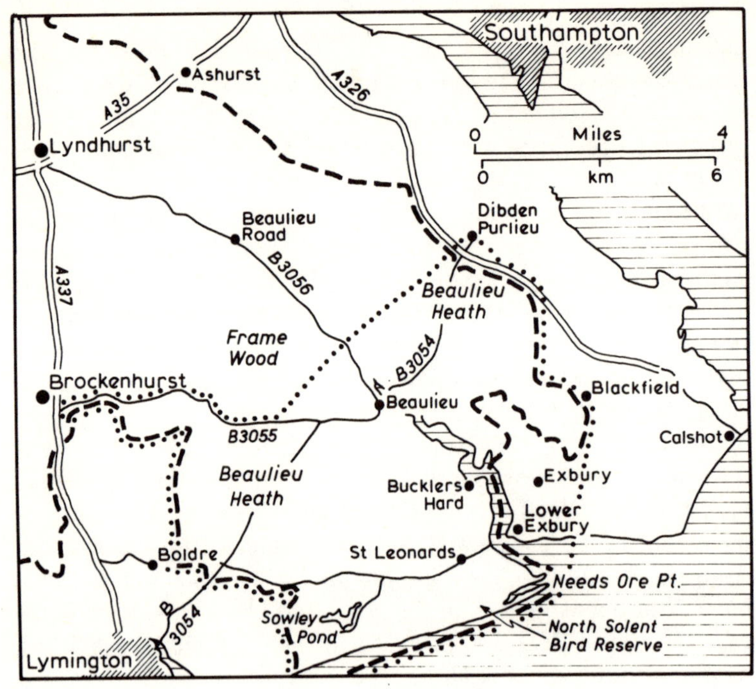

Beaulieu and the South East

4 *Beaulieu and the South East*

'The great bell of Beaulieu was ringing. Far away through the forest might be heard its musical clamour. Peat Cutters on Blackdown and fishers up the Exe heard the distant throbbing. All around the abbey monks were trooping in. Under the long green paved avenues of gnarled oaks and of lichened beeches, the white robed brothers gathered. From the vineyard and the vinepress, from the Ox farm, from the marlpits and salterns, even from the distant iron works of Sowley and the outlying Grange of St Leonards.' Thus wrote Conan Doyle in his story *The White Company*, to evoke the busy and far-flung estates of the monks.

So we too start at Beaulieu, for though the monks have been gone more than four hundred years, these are still feudal lands, owned today by Lord Montagu, and the power of Beaulieu stretches out far and wide.

King John founded the abbey in 1204, granting the Cistercian Order 8,500 acres of rough forest round the shores of a creek, the only building being a small hunting lodge called Beau Lieu, beautiful place. Gathering to themselves a band of lay brothers, the monks cleared the land, set up a system of outlying granges, great barns to store corn, and ran vast flocks of sheep – seventy years after its founding the abbey owned four thousand sheep and a warehouse in Southampton from which wool was shipped to Italy: the monks' own habits were made of undyed wool, hence they were often called the white monks.

Near the head of the creek they raised a church the size of Winchester Cathedral and a vast range of domestic buildings, two gatehouses against the French raids, a refectory and cloisters for study. Although the choir monks spent part of the day in worship and reading, the whole abbey was a hive of industry as lay brothers and their servants cultivated the gardens, tended vineyard and fishponds, baked bread, wove cloth, copied manuscripts – nor were they backward in defending their rights. 'Robert Collyng and Gosse Bredering are plaintiffs of the abbot of Beaulieu that when they were fishing in the sea the abbot with his monks and lay brothers came with swords and sticks, bows and arrows, and other arms and assaulted them … and by force of arms took the boat in which they were fishing and removed it to Beaulieu,' says a thirteenth-century court statement.

A village grew up round the abbey gates: forest people were often resentful of this powerful empire carved from their land: when the abbey tried to extend their demesne, the new walls were thrown down. The abbot was even taken to court. 'It is presented that the abbot of Beaulieu pastured in the forest so many horses, mares, cattle, sheep and other animals that they are ignorant of the numbers … to the injury of the whole district.'

The guide to Beaulieu reproduces in colour some of the buildings as they were before the Dissolution by Henry VIII, but the very best reconstructions are in a small book published in 1952 in which the architect Arthur E. Henderson has drawn intricately detailed views of the huge church from every angle – making it all the more tragic that less remains of Beaulieu now than of almost any abbey in Britain. Very quickly after the Dissolution the central fortress tower and tall gables, arched windows and delicate pinnacles were torn down and the stones shipped off to build coastal defences such as Calshot and Hurst Castles, and the 'cowes', or forts, at Cowes. Later the abbey ruins became a farmyard, but the monks' dining-hall or refectory was retained as parish church, and Thomas Wriothesley, to whom all the estate had been sold, made a dwelling out of the inner gatehouse.

Today the Beaulieu estate is the biggest honeypot in the New Forest, with acres of car-parks among the trees and a range of pleasures, from vintage cars to herb gardens, effortlessly absorbing thousands each summer day. The busiest of all are the mammoth jumble sales devoted to boats in the spring and cars in the autumn – the auto jumble sale attracts over thirty thousand people in two days.

On a sunny June morning we sat on the grass by the creek, fed the ducks and agreed that only the traffic shooting past our backs prevented this being an idyllic spot. On our left sloping oak woods bordered the water; below the wall at our feet the river widened out like a lake – three small boats reflected their own image, swans moved slowly past, aloof.

On our right a jumble of narrow gables and wooden jetties make a picturesque corner; this is the old tidemill built in the seventeenth century and extended in the eighteenth. It was last used by the Norris family to grind cattlefood but is now in a ruinous condition inside. However, the Beaulieu estate has long-term plans to restore it to working order, when funds permit. Many visitors would be interested to see this as there are so few tidemills left, but the project will be fraught with difficulty because the mill backs straight onto the busy road. From the opposite side, we could see five massive sluice gates beneath the road regulating the flow of water into the pond above. It was the releasing of water from the pond which provided power for the mill on an ebb tide.

From here the village street curves up hill, the cottages all warm brown and rust bricks and tiles with dormer windows. Today the whole street smells of blossom, wistaria, lilac and laburnum. Though the village caters for the visitor in a small way, it is on a fairly expensive level – one feels plastic monks are not encouraged. Instead there is hand-made pottery, fine arts – and chocolates.

Five years ago Ruth Liversedge began to experiment with some cooking chocolate to see if she could make her own Easter eggs, just for fun. Today the window is full not only of mouth-watering boxes of home-made chocolates but of all kinds of figures and groups, a mother dog and puppies, the Owl and the Pussycat and tall swans: they are all so beautifully finished that from across the street it looks like a window full of china figures. No wonder they are being sold at London's most prestigious stores – next stop, New York! As in Carisbrooke across the Solent, where the castle entrance is some distance from the village, many thousands must come to the abbey complex who never visit the village itself – thus missing this unusual display.

Opposite the abbey gates, lawns dip to the tide edge, and the roofs of boathouses glimpsed between the trees hint at expensive properties discreetly tucked away. On the fragments of the monks' boundary wall grow little red poppies and yellow stonecrop. Over it we can see the church and Palace House, once the gatehouse with an entrance through its middle, but much rebuilt and enlarged in the 1870s – all so beautifully done in stone, few realize that those narrow gables, tall chimneys and stone mullions are not at least Tudor.

We have come today to see the monastic buildings, since they are truly linked to the forest, but cannot resist taking the monorail which whisks us silently through the treetops, over the model railway pavilion, through the roof of the Transport Museum where we glimpse gleaming rows of vintage cars below, to the Domus, once home to the lay brothers.

Beaulieu never ceases to develop, a key to its commercial success. In 1977 the ground floor of the remaining Domus, once converted into a house for the parson, and the Cellarium with its low-arched ceiling were restored to house the Exhibition of Monastic Life at Beaulieu, which was opened by Sir Arthur Bryant, the eminent historian. Here monks in life-size effigy work at desks or shear sheep: pictures and models show the abbey as a working community, while fragments of carved stone bear testament to the monks' craftsmanship.

This leads to the cloisters, a square of lawn still surrounded by stone walls and archways, the heart of the ruins as it was once the heart of the monastery. Recently they have been planted with beds of all the herbs the monks might have used, both in the kitchen and as medicine, since plants were the only kind then known. Besides the usual pot herbs, there were bright carpets of golden marjoram, pale green starry leaves of lady's mantle and woodruff once laid in linen closets for its fragrance. Nicholas Culpeper, the seventeenth-century herbalist, said, of the next planting, 'lily of the valley strengthens the brain and recruits a week memory', and that lavender cotton 'heals the biting of venemous beasts', perhaps the adders so common in the forest. The cloisters, though roofless walks now, are still sheltered from the world, their old walls warms from the sun with scents of thyme or rosemary drifting on the air. Here was tall, feathery fennel, which our forest herbalist, Juliet de Bairacli Levy, recommends for the eyes, and there is green hellebore bearing long seedpods for it flowers early, once thought a cure for madness.

The church opening out of the cloisters bears little to show it was built as the monks' dining-room except a flight of worn steps up through the thickness of the west wall leading to a lectern from which holy readings would be given during meals. Right up to 1939 this church remained independent of Winchester diocese. Robert Powles, made chaplain in 1886, held that he was really Abbot of Beaulieu.

One day, walking a colt across 'The Holy Ground', then a farmyard, he noticed the animal stumble over a hole; when this was excavated, he and Lord Montagu discovered the lead coffin of Isabella, Duchess of Cornwall, King John's daughter-in-law. Both men became fascinated by the ruins and they set in hand the work which has resulted in the present lay-out of the abbey church foundations.

These at least show the vast scale of the building and the site of the high altar, but the only wall left standing is that which backs onto the cloisters. Though this faces north, it is home to an interesting community of plants including yellow toadflax, wild strawberry, centaury and the very rare, ill-named, common pink. Another plant, winter savory, which resembles a hanging heather but actually belongs to the mint family, grows wild nowhere else in Britain. Alone of all the herbs now to be seen and smelled at Beaulieu, this one could be descended from the monks' own plants, for it was much valued as a medicine. 'Keep it dry by you all year,' said Culpeper, 'if you love yourself and your ease. Quickens the dull spirit in lethargy.' Damp and sunless corners where two walls make an angle are green with flourishing colonies of spleenwort, a delicate black-stemmed fern resembling maidenhair.

Beside the present-day church lies one of the monks' ponds where they bred carp, an old willow trailing its leaves in the still water, a mother coot with three young ones gliding between yellow iris and the pink heads of bistort. When Hudson was at Beaulieu watching swallows skim a pond's surface, he saw a huge pike leap from the water and try – in vain – to snatch one of the birds.

Away from Transporama and even ancient altars, along a lane winding deep into Hartford Wood, we found the Woodland Study Centre set up by the Countryside Education Trust in 1975. Here school children may come and explore the nature trail, dip into ponds, study forestry and monitor air pollution, food chains of predators, various birds nests and skulls, with other activities that vary with the seasons. On this visit we saw adder and grass snake in adjoining tanks, tadpoles and an enormous wasps' nest.

Just outside is a teaching glade with a handy rabbit warren, fenced off, and watchful slinky ferrets in hutches. The whole aim of the centre is to educate children in conservation activities appropriate to the New Forest – there are courses for adults also. For example, one school party had cut wood to size and built a charcoal kiln, while others split hazel rods in the coppice for making wattle fence or learned how to make natural dyes.

Moving north from Beaulieu, we went for a walk in the woods, just to remind ourselves that this is all New Forest ground, but the influence of the abbey is ever present in the names of places. For example, Beufre, from the French *boeuf*, beef, is where they kept their cattle; Bergerie was their sheep farm, and this wood is called Tantony, a corruption of St Antony, because he was the patron saint of swineherds – pigs would have been sent out here in the autumn to live on fallen acorns – the north end in fact is called Pig Bush, misnomer for a pretty wood. Tantany itself offered us the evening shade of noble beeches, great spreading oaks and particularly tall birch.

One of the charms of this forest is the sudden total contrast of country: winding, leafy paths brought us round a bend onto Halfpenny Green, a wide spread of marshy lawn where ponies grazed with their new foals beside them and little bog plants colonized the wettest hollows.

Local Style: Beaulieu Abbey

Hale Church

Minstead Church

Creek Farm and old salt houses

Bramshaw Church

Lymington Harbour

Lymington Town Quay

Moving on southward we came to Hatchet Pond.

Eighteenth-century maps show only pits on this site where marl, a mixture of clay and lime, was dug to fertilize the poor forest soil, but these have long been flooded to form a crescent-shaped pond with one long horn. Few walk far from car-park and picnic area; most of the shore is green and wild with patches of sweet-scented bog myrtle, gorse and birch scrub, even a little pine wood. Out on the shining water a mallard with seven fluffy brown ducklings in line astern swims past a drift of bog-bean raising pale spikes into the air, and martens dip down to drink. Some of the mallard are the biggest we had ever seen, goose size; some of the males moreover had purple head feathers rather than the normal emerald, though the colour is always difficult to identify as the gloss changes with the angle of light. Normal-size coot wearing the distinctive white head shield skulked among the protective thickets of great reed mace, often called bulrushes. In winter, whole flocks of duck, particularly pochard, take refuge here.

Along grassy ditches and hollows by the pond's edge, water mint was in bud, marsh pennywort covered the ground with its green leather buttons, while here and there the prostrate mats of Hampshire purslane shone copper-coloured in the evening sun. Though flourishing here, this is very rare now (three stars in Collins' Guide) and should not be disturbed.

A book written some sixty years ago lists all kinds of rare birds here too, including three kinds of bittern, but no booming disturbed the twilight as we turned for home. Heywood Sumner says that the name Hatchet, met elsewhere in the forest as Holly Hatch, is derived from a hatch gate which used to lead from farm land to heath.

South-west of Hatchet lies a great stretch of Beaulieu Heath, flat and heathery, the horizon bounded by the woods of Hawk Hill to the north, while southward the first hills are the far downs of the Isle of Wight. Ponies wander among the gorse, stonechats perch on the highest branches, chinking – cyclists flit past! For the heath is still criss-crossed with tarmac and concrete, though the airfield has been gone more than twenty-five years: the roads, some of them old runways, are closed to vehicles, so ideal for cyclists, and indeed walkers who need flat going. The very straightness of the roads can be monotonous but one can always wander off onto rabbit tracks, and the vast skyscape lends a feeling of airy space.

In 1910 the New Forest Flying School was established here: this was taken over as a Military Flying School during the 1914-18 War, then retained as a civil landing ground. It was not until the last war that the wide, irregular hexagon of Beaulieu Airfield took shape, with the consequent sprawl of service buildings. After the war it was used as an experimental station for testing gliders, helicopters and parachute drops and finally given up by the Air Ministry in 1960, when the buildings were removed and much of the hard standing broken up into rubble now overgrown with heather, grass and pettywhin.

There is still flying on the heath though: we watched a red and yellow monoplane take off from runway number one, on a practice flight. It was made of polystyrene and balsa wood, with a wing span of four feet. Here a long stretch of concrete has been retained as a flying range for radio-controlled model aircraft: at a club rally a rainbow of little planes, gliders and even helicopters takes the air, each with its own frequency: enthusiasts maintain it is the finest model flying-ground in England.

Round the edge of the heath, the little villages of East Boldre, East End and Norleywood were no end shaken up by the influx of service personnel in both world wars. During the first, a plane crashed onto the roof of East Boldre post office, one of many accidents whose victims lie in the churchyard there. Hatchet Pond was used to test depth charges.

In July 1940, when the war news was at its blackest, SOE, Special Operations Executive, was established and Winston Churchill sent a characteristic message, 'Set Europe ablaze!' SOE was to dispatch agents secretly into enemy-held territory for sabotage operations and to link up with underground organizations already working against the Germans. Secluded Beaulieu became a finishing school for SOE agents. A previous Lord Montagu had built various houses for his own friends on the estate, each so well screened they could not see their neighbours. After six months training the agents came to these – one called 'The House in the Woods' was the officers' mess – for their final course, which was how to survive in enemy territory: the royal gamekeeper was sent down from Sandringham to teach them woodcraft.

Many of these agents eventually flew out from Beaulieu Airfield and were dropped by parachute into Europe, though the small Lysander planes sometimes actually landed, briefly, on enemy soil. In the cloisters of the abbey there is a memorial inscription on the wall: 'To the men and women of the European Resistance secretly trained at Beaulieu to fight their lonely battle against Hitler's Germany ... who here found some measure of the peace for which they fought.'

Today the villages near the airfield are working communities unnoticed by tourists: perhaps a few find Monksmead Studio among the straggle of cottages and bungalows at East Boldre; there you can buy pottery taking its colour from the local clays. There used to be a rope works here until the 1860s, supplying rope to the shipyards at Bucklers Hard: the row of cottages built for the spinners is still here.

Part of East End faces a green: another lane straggles off to a farm. We are on the very edge of the forest now, with a view over cultivated land, but nightingales sing in the neighbouring woods.

Elsewhere in this south-east corner of the forest, the night air is rent by a very different sound, a very loud croaking!

Sometimes near the beginning of this century a resident of Beaulieu with a large garden introduced into it various exotic creatures from abroad, including a group of green tree frogs. Over the years some escaped and formed colonies of their own: some of these seem to have been destroyed by the bitter winter of 1962-3, but they are still flourishing here and there.

At twilight on an evening in early June we sat down by a small pond where newts swam among white-flowered crowfoot and a warbler serenaded the last daylight from a gorse bush. Presently even he was quiet. Now and then little plops came from the water. When we had almost given up, there suddenly sounded a familiar, raucous croak from the bank, answered by another from mid pond, then a third, till the night was loud with a whole cacophony of croaks. Torchlight – which they do not seem to notice – revealed two squatting on low gorse branches; little sucker discs on their feet enable them to climb about. But the most surprising thing is their size. Brilliant emerald green with bright yellow underparts, surely the most beautiful of frogs, each frog is no more than the size of your thumb joint. Should you come upon any of these mighty-voiced midgets, please keep the locality to yourself: such delightful little creatures deserve to thrive in their secret places.

Passing near Round Hill, an overflow campsite on the edge of Beaulieu Heath, only used at such peak times as Bank Holidays, we visited another escape. There, lighting the dark glade of a conifer wood, was a small cluster of rhododendron bushes – not very unusual in the forest you might think, but this was *r. luteum*, with loose clusters of yellow flowers with a heady fragrance drifting far out into the sombre aisles of pine trees.

Of course the place to study rhododendrons is Exbury, so next day we set off down the east bank of the river from our centre at Beaulieu.

William Mitford built Exbury House in the eighteenth century, replacing an older building. The estate was later owned by the Forster family, Harry marrying a Montagu and so linking the neighbouring demesnes. Lionel de Rothschild, of the banking family, was also a friend of the Montagus – he and John Montagu were co-owners of a speedboat *Yarrow-Napier* which broke the world record. When Inchmery House on the river mouth was put up for sale, Lionel was quick to buy this property near his friend. During the 1914 war both the Forster boys were killed: their father, Harry, now Lord Forster, decided to sell the whole estate and moved to Lepe.

Lionel de Rothschild bought Exbury, rebuilding the house to a large extent though keeping its Georgian look, and moved in during 1921: he also built cottages for his workers, but it was his work, and that of his son Edmund, on the grounds which has made them world famous. Lionel had a consuming passion for rhododendrons, so an army of labourers, 150, supervised by seventy-five gardeners, set about preparing the grounds. These had to be cleared of scrub and in some cases forest, though the finer trees were left to provide shelter and shade. Plant-hunting at this time was a new craze with the travel freedom of peacetime returned. Lionel financed expeditions to the Himalayas to bring back new varieties and was heard to say, 'Why plant one when a bank of fifty would look better?'

The garden, with two acres of greenhouses, was not complete till 1935. Not content with mere planting, Lionel made innumerable cross-breedings to establish new varieties; all his family have plants named after them; he particularly yearned to breed a clear yellow. Sadly *R. Hawk Crest*, his greatest success in that colour, did not flower till after his death in 1942.

During the war Exbury House was requisitioned by the Royal Navy and commissioned at HMS *Mastodon*, one of the bases where the invasion of France was planned. When Edmund, who inherited, came back in 1946, it was to a wilderness of bramble and thorn, overgrown shrubs and decaying Nissen huts. The bees, though, had continued the work of hybridizing, and there were many new varieties to be listed. Edmund was determined to restore the gardens as a memorial to his father. However, at this time even bankers needed extra funds. To help with the restoration and upkeep, the grounds were opened to the public and plants put on sale. The prosperous sixties and seventies provided a market for young trees: thousands of these were sold to line motorways, new estates and London parks. With the recession and consequent decline of wholesale markets, there are plans for a new approach.

On a sunny morning in early June, Exbury seemed a far cry from recession and market place, a world of colour and fragrance, green lawns and shaded pools, little winding paths and majestic, ancient trees. Though cars had already overflowed onto the grass, Exbury's 250 acres had absorbed all the visitors so well that each might take away an impression of tranquillity, gaze down vistas of flowers blooming seemingly for him alone.

We began our walk along the Bridal Path between cascades of white blossom hanging from King George, a scented rhododendron, white azaleas, and red *R. Leo*, the first we were to see of many hybrids named after family members. The banks of middle pond glowed with evergreen azaleas in brilliant fire colours, orange, flame, pink, yellow, and every one reflected again in the clear, dark water. From here a path leads down through the huge primrose-yellow flowerheads of *R. Fortune* in the early flowering Winter Garden to a viewpoint over Beaulieu River looking toward Bucklers Hard and a rose garden planted in memory of Edmund Rothschild's wife, Elizabeth.

Lover's Lane, Witcher's Wood, named after the gypsies who once lived there, the pink and white magnolias of Yard Wood, the tall cedars of the Glade and candelabra primulas of the Bog Garden, Augustinii Corner all blue and yellow because those are the de Rothschild racing colours – one needs a whole day to wander among them all, explore inviting little paths branching from the main and enjoy the sheer variety of plants, by no means all rhododendrons. There is even the largest rock garden in Europe, only now in process of being reclaimed from years of neglect and planted with dwarf species.

After all this grace and colour we were taken to see a large area of derelict outhouses – because Exbury moves on all the time and this is the site of its next development, a new entrance, car-park and plant retail centre (for which there will be no admission fee), of course specializing in rhododendrons, camellias and azaleas.

Edmund de Rothschild's son Nicholas had produced a video, *The Glory of the Garden*, in which James Mason tells the story of the founding of Exbury Gardens – this has helped to spread their fame around the world.

Exbury village has moved. The monks of Beaulieu built a chapel near the mouth of the river, and a hamlet grew up at what is now Lower Exbury, but William Mitford, when lord of the manor, built a new church and village nearer to Exbury House – the church, dating from 1827, is now almost opposite the gardens entrance. The old chapel was pulled down, though a bell from it hangs in the tower, its chalice is still used at communion services, and some of its stones were built into the walls.

We opened the south door onto a plain interior, but the eye is immediately drawn to the chapel opposite where lies a striking full-length bronze effigy of Alfred Forster, the youngest son of the manor. Beside it on the wall hangs a memorial tablet to his brother John, also killed in the war. Lord Forster decided to make the larger bronze the central feature of a new memorial chapel, and this was added in 1927, together with the tower above it. Lord Forster left Lepe to become Governor General of Australia but returned there eventually; he and his wife also have a memorial in the chapel.

Other wall tablets bear the name of Mitford. When the family built the church, there was a gallery with a fireplace at the west end for their private use, but this was removed during extensive alterations early this century, which also gave it the high, vaulted roof. Today, as at Boldre, new benches, pedestals and tables of forest oak are all the work of local craftsmen, continuing the tradition laid down by the monks of Beaulieu who built the original Exbury chapel with their own hands.

Exbury village is still small, with a tidy row of shops and the same cared-for air as Beaulieu, its equally feudal neighbour. Further south a track leads down to the site of the old church, and a footpath straggles along the tide edge by clumps of sea pink and sea spinach. Here at Lower Exbury was a brickworks making the yellow bricks used in the construction of the church and also of Inchmery House. This has gardens stretching along the shore and wide views across the mouth of Beaulieu River and the Solent to the Isle of Wight. Exbury House is used for meetings and concerts, but Inchmery is now the country home of this branch of the family.

The lane leads on through fields and copse, over the Dark Water, skirting the oaks of Kings Copse Inclosure to Blackfield. The actual forest boundary is marked down the middle of Beaulieu River, so that in Exbury we were just outside, yet as we come back into the forest proper at Blackwell Common, the view is all of great chimneys and pylons for we are on the edge of the vast industrial complex lining Southampton Water, Fawley Oil Refinery, Marchwood Power Station and the rest. Hurriedly we turn west, escaping back onto heathland, and in incredibly short time are back in oak-bowered Beaulieu.

Next day we set out to walk down river to Bucklers Hard: a discreet wooden fingerpost points the way since the Beaulieu estate does not advertise the lower village – people who really want to visit it will find it, and they are as many as Bucklers Hard can comfortably cope with: it is the abbey complex which can absorb large crowds.

Of those who find the beginning of the path, some will be put off by the first few hundred yards, through the pub's car-park, along a very rough gravel track past houses and, what's more, swerving away from the river, but once into the fields it is a delightful 2½-mile potter.

A meadow yellow with buttercups slopes down to the shining, lake-wide river, oak woods on the far bank sloping down to the shore with just a glimpse of roof here and there tucked away. Along the path grow moon daisies, sorrel and clovers, while drifts of fragrance move on the summer air from hawthorns still white with may blossom.

Part of the east bank just below Beaulieu used to be known as Factory Meadow as ropes were made there.

Where the path crosses a small shady creek, ragged robin, like torn campions, have colonized a marshy patch, with the still curled heads of new bracken and sky-blue speedwell. Amongst them we find butterfly and spotted orchids, not the rarest of their family but any orchid adds lustre to the day.

Skirting a cornfield we are for a while out of sight of the river, though never out of sound – a flock of oyster catchers is piping and calling in their frantic-seeming way. More hawthorns almost hide a half-ruined brickworks behind a cottage, a tall gable of rust brick, a chimney and further down a beehive-shaped kiln, all overgrown with Virginia creeper, with baby turkeys running about in the long grass. The brickyard was opened in 1790 and prospered till the 1920s.

Turning down a lane off the main path, where twayblades grew on the shady side, we came to a little grass knoll and jetty where a mallard with seven ducklings waddled about between a few hauled-up dinghies. This is Bailey's Hard, where the very first naval vessel was built on Beaulieu River: she was the *Salisbury*, launched in 1698 and captured by the French five years later. The last warship was a minesweeper, built here by Husbands of Southampton during the last war – such recent industry comes as a surprise all among the ducks and dinghies.

Returning to the main path, we skirt a holiday hamlet, chalets built up on stilts with outside staircases, hollow beneath for boat or car; since they were built, the copse has edged in close, screening the river view but lending the atmosphere of living in a high nest, like a rook.

Keeping Copse is a mixed wood of birch oak and hazel with a few white-flowered wild service trees, planted about 1820 to take the place of oak felled for shipbuilding. A sea breeze stirs the branches, and the wood floor, green with new bracken, is spangled with sunlight. Cow wheat grows here and there like a small yellow snapdragon; blackcaps and a thrush are singing overhead, a distant cuckoo calling, yet the wood is full of hazards! From almost every branch, it seems, hang the caterpillars of the geometer moths on hardly visible gossamer swings, and most just at hair level!

The trees fall back, there are boats ahead and we are almost in Bucklers Hard. On our right is a thatched cottage built in 1760 by George, Duke of Montagu, as a sea-water bath-house for his son.

The best way to understand Bucklers Hard is to walk up the hill between the rows of russet brick and tiled cottages to the Maritime Museum and there study a model of the village as it was in its shipbuilding heyday – it is precisely dated Friday 3 June 1803, three days before the launching of HMS *Euryalus*.

John Montagu created Bucklers Hard: it was to be a port to rival Southampton, called Montagu Town. A wide road was cleared and built down through the woods with a quay at its foot. Duke John was governor of two islands in the West Indies which he intended to colonize, and build up a large sugar-importing trade at Montagu Town. But his expedition was sent packing by the French and had to return home: Montagu Town was never built and the quay was used as a timber wharf until the Wyatt brothers obtained the commission to build a warship there, Britain being at war with France again and the naval dockyards overworked. So shipyard and village began to grow; with the coming of that marvellous shipbuilder Henry Adams, it began to be of real importance, launching more than fifty great warships in some eighty years, and merchant vessels too.

So here on the model is the wide road for the timber wagons sloping to the river and the dormered cottages facing each other across it just as they are today, but dwarfing all are the two warships on their slipways at the foot of the hill, *Euryalus*, decked, masted and painted ready for launch, with the much bigger *Swiftsure* beside her, half built on stocks – seventy-four guns she was to carry. All down the street lie piles of timber, with more seasoning in fields behind the village, bringing home the huge amount of wood, chiefly oak, felled in the forest for Bucklers Hard alone. *Swiftsure* would have needed some sixty acres.

The museum offers many elegant models of ships built here – and much else. Recently extended, it now leads into a complete re-creation of the bar of the New Inn in the eighteenth century: lantern light flickers over the locals with their beer, a dog sleeps on a settle in a muted hum of voices, and all so real-seeming that a shiver runs down your back. Henry Adams is still at work too in the window of his master builder's house, now a hotel, overlooking the river.

One could easily miss the chapel, since it is the front room of one of the cottages, originally the cobbler's shop and afterwards used as a schoolroom. Then the Rev. Powles, who, as we have seen, regarded himself as Abbot of Beaulieu, began to hold occasional services there for elderly locals unable to travel.

When young Peter Rylands came to Beaulieu Airfield, he was befriended by Lady Poole of Buckler's Wood. While he was only eighteen, Ryland's plane came down in the sea off the mouth of the river and he was drowned. As a memorial to him, Lady Poole 'set the chapel in order', as a silver plaque commemorates. On a summer's day it is dark and cool, lined with panelling from Ladycross Lodge in the forest. About thirty-five people can worship beneath its low ceiling or view its treasures; a dark, ancient wooden statue of the Virgin Mary, the memorial to Lady Poole and her son, and a silver crucifix from Beaulieu are among them. The guidebook is by Elizabeth Goudge, the famous novelist, who set a trilogy of her books in a house she called Damerosehay somewhere on the edge of the nearby marshes.

It is difficult to explore these and the river mouth since much of the land is now private, so we took to the water, in fact to *Swiftsure* – the modern version, that is, more like a floating greenhouse than a boat so there is none of that splendid wind-through-the-hair feeling, but still the visibility is good. She makes excursion trips down river all season from a small pier beside the present-day boatyard which builds yachts of so opulent a size that the cars parked below them look like toy models.

Swiftsure slips out into the river, the green wooded banks of Salternshill slide past under a blue sky with white puffs of cloud and a flash of gulls' wings. An inlet to starboard is a small harbour built by the first Lord Montagu for breeding oysters, but used in the last war for the construction of the revolutionary floating docks called Mulberry Harbour which were towed across to France after the invasion of Normandy: the whole river was packed with landing craft before D-Day. Now the oyster trade is being revived.

Shelduck fly over, a flock of geese graze the Exbury mudflats: there is some concern that the spartina grass, which binds the mud into these banks, is dying back and no one is yet sure of the cause. The woods fall away revealing pasturelands, cattle grazing and Gins Farm. Here the monks had a gin or winch for loading barges with wool from their vast sheepruns and salt from the salt pans higher up the river; now the inlet provides headquarters for the Royal Southampton Yacht Club.

Swiftsure swept round in a wide curve and sped us back to Bucklers Hard without reaching the river mouth at Needs Oar, so we would go on foot. The lanes behind the village wind through fields and woods preserved as shooting coverts: male pheasants resplendent in bronze with touches of red and green take off with maximum fuss as if they'd never flown before, while their duller wives and small brown partridge skulk about the ferny banks.

However many times we had come this way before, the sight of St Leonard's Barn on a curve of the lane never fails to fill us with wonder, the huge stone gable looming high above the road all fringed today with red valerian. The monks built this great storehouse, over two hundred feet long, the largest in Britain. Today its end gables remain and some of the walls, patched with yellow stonecrop. Jackdaws fly in and out of the ventilation holes. Inside stands a normal-size barn with lichen-sploshed tile roof, in present-day use. By contrast, in the grounds of St Leonard's Grange behind stands the ruin of a tiny chapel, a west gable, the shape of an east window all draped with ivy; this was only used of course when the monks and lay brothers could not reach the mother church at Beaulieu.

Joan Begbie, who wrote a book about the New Forest in the 1930s, tells a curious tale about St Leonard's. She wanted to visit the chapel and, as the owners were away, talked to the gardener. 'The gardener said that there was an underground passage from the Grange to Beaulieu Abbey; but no one knows now where the entrance lies. In his grandfather's youth it was possible to get into the passage from an opening down by the river … When a lad he and a party of his more adventurous friends tried to explore it. They had to go by boat because the tunnel was half full of water and they carried candles. However, they were forced to turn back as the foul air first turned the candle flames an unhealthy blue, then extinguished them altogether.'

We were going 'down by the river', though not in search of secret tunnels. The North Solent Nature Reserve covers six miles of the Beaulieu River, most of which we had already traversed on foot and by boat, from the millpond behind the Abbey to Gins Farm, but it also includes the mouth from Gins to Needs Ore and four miles of adjoining Solent Coast for which one needs a permit from the Beaulieu Estate office since these are important breeding grounds for seabirds and wildfowl.

We set off down the lane opposite St Leonard's Barn not only with our permits but with the reserve's warden. A great storm in 1952 threw up a long shingle spit which forms a sheltered lagoon, ideal wader country. The Isle of Wight hills lay along the southern horizon, a tern fell from the blue sky, a flash of white sploosh into the water and up again, a shining sand eel in his beak. Yellow-horned poppy was in bud along the shingle edge, among the glaucous blue leaves of sea holly, the breeze bringing a clamour of distant gulls. Now and then yacht sails glided past beyond the spit, adding a touch of white or red to this serene seascape.

Actually the yachts, or their owners, are a menace to the reserve, often without the least intention. A boat may land for the kids to pick up shells – and they unwittingly trample on a dozen nests of little tern, for the nest is a mere scrape and the eggs are camouflaged to match the shingle: one thoughtless picnic can wreck a colony of sandwich tern or oyster catcher. North Solent is the first reserve in Britain able to impose a £1,000 fine for illegal landing during the nesting season. Yachts must be held responsible for at least some of the trash thrown into the Solent: at the last clean-up of the North Solent shore, two lorry loads of plastic rubbish were taken away.

The birds have other enemies to contend with. Rats are trapped in early spring but inevitably some survive to prey on eggs and chicks. Surprisingly, grey squirrels come down out of the forest at nesting time, have sometimes been caught out by spring tides and sit it out on isolated tussocks till the waves retreat. Hawks attack from the air. Nevertheless, the warden felt that man was by far the most dangerous predator, and the reserve desperately needed its new fining power, situated as it is near the huge marina in Lymington River and others in Southampton Water and the Isle of Wight.

We walked out to Needs Ore, the point right at the mouth of Beaulieu River with a small boathouse on the end for a yacht club. Members had lately been worried by the ringed plover, which had taken to nesting on the bare ground where cars were usually parked. Someone had the bright idea of setting an old wire milk crate over each nest. This worked splendidly, mother birds not turning a feather at having to thread the wires to return to their eggs, and members able to see what spots to avoid.

From this exhilarating headland with sea all round, you can sometimes see a deer swimming up the river – and always there is the scolding and crying of the black-headed gulls out on Gull Island, twelve thousand pairs nest out there, making it the biggest colony in the British Isles. Sandwich tern flittered down to their nests on the crest of the shingle bank among lovely piping cries of redshank. Between the tufts of sea pink a ringed plover threaded her way followed by two tiny brown chicks like overgrown bumblebees – one fell over a stone and skimmed over the ground like a clockwork toy to catch up with mum; presently they returned to the safety of their milk crate.

We walked back past the coastguard cottages, now weekend homes for Londoners. North Solent is the first reserve in Hampshire to make special provision for handicapped birdwatchers, providing a hide accessible by wheelchair with viewing slot at the right level.

We visited the Norman Pullen Hide, which overlooks a narrow freshwater lake sheltered by gorsy banks out of sight of the sea, a particular haven for ducks, in fact dug out for them. Little grebe pottered about making friendly sounds rather like giggling; further west the showy shelduck were having a preening and bathing session; tufted duck slid down into the quiet water past brilliant spikes of purple loosestrife, and coot peered out from the reeds, keeping their young ones discreetly hidden away. Not so the mother mallard who cruised past with seven ducklings astern – the eighth kept getting lost on the wrong side of the pond; whenever she managed to round him up, another chick would be missing. When a crow sailed over, she fussed them all into the bank till he went off and a few little tern flew over, seeming to dance on the air for the joy of it.

Turning inland again along quiet lanes through pastures and oak copses, we came to one last sheet of water, Sowley Pond. Only a small part of it is visible from the road, for long arms curve away out of sight, deeply wooded and inaccessible on private estate land. South Leigh, as it was then called, was used to restock the monks' fish ponds at Beaulieu. A local legend told how the monks took their gold statue of the Virgin secretly by night and threw it into Sowley Pond, rather than let it fall into the hands of the King's Commissioners, on the eve of the Dissolution. So in 1907, when it was proposed to drain the pond (in order to remove the coarse fish and stock it with trout), there was some excitement as to what might be found there. But no treasure came to light, alas. It would have been fitting to find some trace of Beaulieu here, since the monks were responsible for the existence of Sowley. In 1280 a case was brought at Winchester: 'It is presented that the Abbot of Beaulieu has newly made a certain pond outside the king's wood of Suthle, and has enclosed a certain water so that it has overflowed upon the king's land for five furlongs in length to the damage of the forest and all the country and by the water they destroyed the road to a marlpit to the damage of the vill of Badesle.'

Under dark pines the lake shines in the evening light; long-tailed tits flit through the fringing oaks, and a moorhen trills an alarm – we are glad the abbot was acquitted, and the birds must be grateful too. It is a great duck haven in winter, when hundreds of wigeon, pochard and teal fly in, with Canada geese also, and sometimes a great northern diver makes a home here.

Difficult to imagine, with a thrush singing and an occasional plop of water vole, that this was once the noisiest place in the forest! For there was once an iron-smelting works here, the iron ore being brought up from the beaches, especially those beneath Hengistbury Head. This was still working in 1810. The great forge hammer gave rise to the New Forest proverb. 'There will be rain when Sowley hammer is heard', and this applied over a wide district.

So monks and ironworkers alike are gone, but the herons have moved in. Scots pine clothe the far bank, a gentle rise, and there is much flapping and toing and froing on ponderous grey wings. Through binoculars we can see four nests in one pine, each with a tall sentinel bird beside it, while others fish on the bank below, silent and still, the colour of twilight.

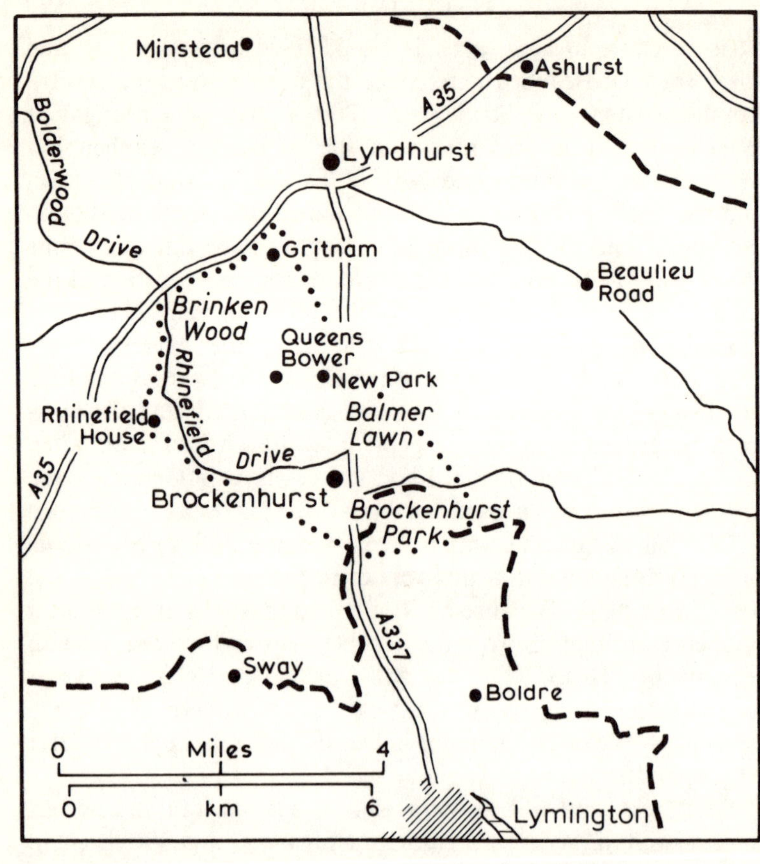

Brockenhurst and its Western Woods

5 *Brockenhurst and its Western Woods*

Turn a corner of the path and you come suddenly upon a tree on either side soaring to such height they take your breath away – the Tall Trees walk was laid out by the Forestry Commission so that the Rhinefield Ornamental Drive can be enjoyed on foot, away from the road.

The Drive was originally a mere track leading to a forest lodge. In 1859 many specimen trees, some only recently brought into England, were planted alongside, together with rhododendrons and other shrubs. Though only surfaced in 1938, this is one of the most popular motor routes in the whole New Forest, especially when the rhododendrons are in bloom – no heavy traffic is allowed.

Of course the trees can only really be appreciated on foot. We began at the north end of the Drive with Brock Hill Walk, which led gently up through spreading oak and beech to a little knoll with a view deep down into the woods, taking its name from the badger sett on the top. There were a few holes to be seen, but even the most recent had cobwebs across its mouth: plainly the badgers didn't care for such a public home, at least in summer. The Forestry Commission regularly monitor the badger population, taking care not to upset them when planting is going on and even providing special gates, like large puss-flaps, when necessary.

The tallest tree on the summit, a Douglas fir, had been struck by lightning, almost cut in half by a great black furrow from top to bottom, but part was still gallantly growing.

The path circled back through mixed woods, the air rank from a group of stinkhorns by the path, their caps just ripe, attracting flies from all round. Where the floor was bare of bracken, we could see many cones chewed to the core by squirrels, and everywhere wood ants were struggling over dead leaves and pine needles, carrying burdens as big as themselves back to the nest.

This half-mile stroll having led back to the car-park, we go on to the Tall Trees Walk through groves of lofty Douglas firs, their bark so deeply wrinkled as to resemble ropes and shaded lovely subtle colours, purple to palest green above the dark wood floor: this is transformed when we reach a stretch of larches, for their lighter shade allows a green carpet of grass to flourish. Here a young beech has been forced into corkscrew shape by a honeysuckle bine, and another will never grow straight since a grey squirrel has stripped off the bark down one side.

The path is surfaced and level, with small bridges now and then, suitable like Bolderwood for wheel- and pushchair; the walker can stroll at leisure, reading information posts which describe and identify outstanding trees such as silver fir, deodar and the tallest black spruce in Britain.

On this summer morning the air is full of the fragrance of pines. We have come to a cross ride and there are the tallest of all, two Wellingtonias, the one on the left with slender pyramidal branches reaching more than 150 feet. In their native California, Wellingtonias can reach twice this height, but our English winds will probably slow growth now these specimens have outtopped all the other trees. Passing a grove of Corsican pine, so tall and straight that their seed is specially prized for cultivation, we came to another outstanding tree of Rhinefield, the *Sequoia sempervirens*, or redwood, with its distinctive orange-brown bark, named after an Indian chief called Sequoyah, son of a Cherokee princess and a German settler.

Here we diverted, turning right down the Blackwater Walk to visit the Arboretum. Originally a wood of scrubby oak and Douglas fir, this was felled and cleared (the army being called in to blow up some of the huge stumps), surrounded by deer fencing and replanted with special trees in 1959 and 60, a hundred years after the original planting of Rhinefield. Well spaced out in mown grass are little trees which may one day replace fallen giants, rowan, locust tree, dragon spruce with seagreen needles, whitebeam, showing its silvery undersides when the breeze blows, and many others.

Back along the Blackwater Walk we appreciated its name – the river flows dark from its peat bed higher up, and spruce met overhead, casting so deep a shadow not even moss grew on the forest floor, though a goldcrest sang out its tiny high notes. Crossing the Drive, we began to circle back and came upon a large pit, locally known as the Elephant's Grave.

By the seventeenth century an enormous amount of timber in the forest had been felled for shipbuilding or destroyed by deer, so in 1698 an Act was passed allowing the Crown to inclose 6,000 acres. To bring home to us the enormous task of inclosing this acreage by hand and fencing against the deer, the Forestry Commission have here reconstructed the original boundary of Rhinefield, inclosed 1700. A ditch five feet deep is topped by a six-foot bank of earth, surmounted in its turn by a strong fence of oak palings. Banks and ditches can be seen everywhere in the forest but eroded and leaf-filled they do not make the same impression as this new stretch.

Today there are 16,000 acres inclosed, though they are not always the same woods. One in need of re-planting may be inclosed this year while another of similar acreage is thrown open when the trees are grown beyond the stage where they can be harmed by grazing animals. The Verderers' Inclosures already discussed are in addition to these.

Returning to the car-park, we passed some other, smaller pits. These are old bomb craters; the Germans made several attempts to burn down the forest since it was a vital source of timber. In 1944 it provided a vast hiding-place for vehicles, troops and stores being concentrated along the south coast for the invasion of Europe – all of which seemed far away as we leant against an oak bole listening to the song of a thrush.

Rhinefield House, at the end of the drive, was originally a forest lodge, the Master Keeper's residence. In 1628 the Earl of Holland granted a sum of money to the Woodward for work on Great Rynefield Lodge, as it was then called, the land round the house later being used as a tree nursery. Later, in the nineteenth century, it was leased to Mabel Walker, who had inherited a fortune from brewing and mining in the Midlands. She proceeded to pull down the old house. She also married at this time and on her honeymoon with Lieutenant Commander Munro fell in love with various buildings round Europe. On her return, now known as Mrs Walker-Munro, she incorporated their various styles into the new mansion being built at Rhinefield, notably a room copied from the Alhambra in Granada, a birthday present for her husband. The old nurseries were laid out as formal gardens, some of the 1859 plantings being allowed to grow on.

After the widowed Mrs Walker-Munro died in 1934, the house became a commune, then a school. Mr Oliver Cutts, a later owner found the grounds a wilderness and the house dilapidated; after much restoration it was opened as a restaurant, specializing in Merrie England Banquets.

Now it is once again in new hands. Coming round a curve of the drive we came suddenly upon Rhinefield, its front dominated by a massive stone tower like a Norman church, flanked by Tudor-style wings with stone mullions and tall brick chimneys, while the top-storey dormers and beams seem to recall half-timbered cottages. A hundred years have weathered its stones: framed in Wellingtonias and redwoods, it makes a beautiful picture, never mind the mix of styles.

The tall window of the Great Hall looks down a long vista, across the grounds and away over the forest to the south east: the Forestry Commission is not allowed to plant high-growing trees along any of the three vistas since this would block the view – Christmas trees are grown there now which will not top six feet before being cut.

As we walked out onto the lawns, three fallow deer were grazing the north-east vista. The gardens are laid out with stone balustrades, fountains, urns and banks of rhododendrons, but what takes the eye are the long canal lakes, once part of a formal Italian garden from which a few scraggy yew bushes remain. The lakes are covered with red and white water-lilies, their flat leaves sheltering the biggest ornamental fish we had ever seen, three kinds of carp, buttercup yellow and every shade of orange, with blue and silver koi from Japan, all cruising among the lily stems.

Inside, the house has just been redecorated and is open as a hotel, the dark panelled Great Hall and its carved galleries re-echoing to the sound of the Orchestrion on the floor above, an amazing cross between a cinema and a fairground organ, reproducing dozens of different instruments and shaking the house with its rendering of 'Edelweiss' – when it was installed the locals maintained it could be heard three miles away!

The next room has a beautiful gilded plaster ceiling, the dining-room displays an intricately carved stone overmantel of a battle scene against the Armada, but the most extraordinary feature of Rhinefield has to be the Alhambra Room: it is like being shut inside a jewel case. Quite small and lit by dim reddish light from a copper lamp in the dome above, walls and floor gleam with gold, ruby, emerald and lapis lazuli blue. The floor is deep red mosaic, walls and dome are covered in beaten copper surrounding rose windows, stars in Venetian glass and lattices through which the women of the harem would have peered, in a Moorish palace.

On a mundane level there are also grilles for the air-conditioning, hot or cold, controlled in the Walker-Munros' time by a great gas engine in the cellars, for beneath Rhinefield's imposing three storeys lies another, then filled by train loads of coal from Mrs Walker-Munro's coalmines in the Midlands. The basement is so vast it already holds a modern central heating plant and a freezer room, with plans for jacuzzis and a swimming-pool.

Leaving Rhinefield and moving toward Brockenhurst, we stopped at Puttles Bridge, where a small car-park for walkers gives access to the Ober Water Walk, an undemanding riverside potter, through old Scots pines and little new self-seeded ones, birch and bracken all along beside the Ober which rises at Backley Plain and joins the Lymington River near Bolderford Bridge. When we sat down on a fallen oak, a wood warbler sang out from a birch, and from the canopy overhead came the busy July hum of insects.

Further on we crossed the river by a wooden footbridge – there are several to vary the length of walk – and found a young magpie squawking for his mother, lately fledged from an untidy nest in a nearby pine. The river slips along between winding, ferny banks through a green shade, a quiet, peaceful retreat, the trees thinning on our left, opening out onto bogland. Once a year though the river is all agog. In late autumn, sea trout swim up river to spawn, waiting for a downpour of rain to raise the water level. They crowd to a gravelly stretch, threshing their tails with such energy you can easily hear the stones crunching. Having made a depression, they lay their eggs. In the shadow of a fallen tree that made a natural bridge, we glimpsed three resident brown trout, though the minnows were not to be seen that day.

The path leads out towards Whitefield Moor. During the last war the eastern part was ploughed up and used to grow cereal crops: over the whole forest some thousand acres of grassland were ploughed up, on the strict understanding that they would be returned to improved grazing land once the emergency was over. So in 1948 Whitefield was reploughed and sown with clover, sheep's fescue and other grasses, providing even today a better pasture than the unimproved lawns, as the number of ponies, foals and cattle grazing bore evidence. Grazed short and brown from the summer's drought, it appeared from the car-park bare of botanic interest, yet once out among the ponies, we found pink centaury, white eyebrights, tiny blue milkworts, hawkbits and enough birdsfoot trefoil to tempt a silver-studded blue butterfly.

Whitefield Moor is a spacious grandstand for watching the ponies' mating rituals. Each stallion gathers about him a harem of mares, a dozen or more, and takes up a territory. If another stallion crosses its invisible boundary line, there will be trouble: a charging stallion is an awesome sight, neck held low, eyes rolling, hooves pounding the turf! After the mating season the mares stay in a loose group, seldom wandering very far from their release point. Stallions are usually moved to a different part of the forest after three years to prevent in-breeding. The foals are born in late spring, adding their leggy, infant charm to the forest picture at bluebell time.

All forest car-parks have notices forbidding the feeding of ponies, since this encourages them to haunt roads in the hope of titbits and so put themselves at risk of being knocked down – the figures are horrifying, sometimes three or four ponies killed in one week, and more injured. It really should not need a penalty of £20 to stop people feeding them.

But the ponies being such a well-loved feature of the forest landscape, motorists, especially those with children, will often stop just to pet them, and this is dangerous in two ways: it still encourages ponies towards roads, and it also puts the motorist himself in danger of a nasty kick! These are wild, unbroken ponies, basically after food, not caresses, and when food is not forthcoming, they will take revenge.

The south-western fringe of Brockenhurst is known as 'The Weirs' though no one seems to know why. There was a large pond there, drained in the 1860s but this would hardly have had a weir since it did not flow anywhere. A drainage channel first put in by the Forestry Commission is called 'The Weir' on present-day ordnance maps but the name is much older than the drain. The Weirs were once looked upon as a separate village, known as rough and wild! There were constant feuds at Brockenhurst School between the locals and the Weirs gang.

South Weirs – that is, south of a line of alders marking the drainage channel – is a scatter of houses along one side of a track all looking out over a wide, heathy hollow to distant woods. We had come to see Harry, a typical forest commoner who had lived here all his life in a thatched cob cottage, walls two feet thick.

Traditionally the commoner had six rights, though these belong to the house rather than the person, and not all houses could claim all six rights. The most important of course was that which enabled him to turn out cattle or ponies in the forest all the year round. Secondly he could depasture pigs in the autumn to eat up acorns and other nuts – this is called common of mast. The right of estover entitles him to an amount of wood for fuel, though a house with this right must date at least in part from Tudor times. The other three are little used now, the right to pasture sheep, common of marl – that is, to dig clay for laying on arable land, and common of turbary, the cutting of turf or peat.

Harry shares a Jersey house cow with his neighbour, keeps a pig from time to time for meat and always has a few hens scratching about the small yard. He does not keep cattle any more but runs twenty ponies and foals on the forest, exercising his commoner's right, though he still has to pay an annual fee for each one – currently £10. His young stallion had just been inspected. This is done at two years old and again at five, when it would be moved by the Verderers to another part of the forest to prevent inbreeding. Harry preferred to sell his ponies privately whenever possible, for riding or children's pets. Selling them at Beaulieu Road pony sales, you risked them going to the 'meat boys', he said, and ending up as pet food. Harry reckoned that many who went to the sales looking for a child's riding pony ended up with poor stock, thinking they were getting a bargain. At the August sales, foals may only be sold with their mothers. By the autumn they can be sold alone.

The cattle grazing in front of the cottage had been brought here from Beaulieu, because springs in the ground beyond kept the runnel flowing and the grass green however little rain fell. Harry maintained that ponies did particularly well in dry weather since areas of bog land previously out of bounds became hard enough for them to walk on and graze, providing a more nutritious mix of plants than the forest lawns.

As to the forest as a whole, he thought it a mess, undrained and overgrown with furze to what it used to be. He remembered when a keeper and a few men with a drum of water on a cart would burn off two or three hundred acres a day, never setting fire to anyone's fence and working only in winter months so as not to harm birds on the nest.

'There's too many people wants too many different things, you see. Some wants butterflies, some wants caravans and some wants they dragons, and between them all, nothing gets done.' (He meant dragon*flies*.)

Harry had always made his living off the forest, supplementing his income by seasonal work such as haymaking, or driving a tractor for the Forestry Commission. Now in his sixties, needing to take things steady, he has found a less energetic way. A big brick outhouse was lined with hutches full of Dutch white rabbits being bred for the table. Fat, placid and expectant, they regarded us with pink eyes, occasionally drew down a pink-lined ear and cleaned it. When the young ones weighed around five pounds, they were sent off to be processed for a famous supermarket chain.

Even Harry could not tell us how North and South Weirs acquired their names; nor could his neighbour, a New Forest Agister.

This is an ancient office originally meaning one who collected dues from those without Forest Right, who grazed cattle or ponies there. For many years the fees were collected by the Lord Warden's steward, so the title Agister went out of use. Then in 1877 the Court of Verderers was reconstituted, to look after the welfare of animals on the forest, and the name Agister revived. In 1912 the Agister asked for a rise in salary. This was refused, but they were given instead their now distinctive uniform of boots, breeches and dark green coats.

Today there are three paid Agisters, helped by half a dozen voluntary Agisters – commoners who can be called upon in time of need. Their work is to supervise the clipping of tails which shows that animals are legally depastured, collect the marking fees and generally oversee that all stock is kept in the best condition possible. The problems they have to face include hit-and-run drivers, cattle-rustling, rogue dogs and the feeding problems caused by hard winters, when the public are quick to ring up with accusing stories of starving ponies and cattle.

On the whole the forest animals are hardy breeds, and this must be true of the Agisters also, for the present Crier to the Court has been in office since 1947.

Leaving South Weirs we come to Brockenhurst village.

In the thirteenth century William Spileman held Brockenhurst by virtue of finding litter for the king's bed and forage for his horse when he came to hunt in the forest. A hundred years later John de Grimstead held it by virtue of providing a horseman for twenty days in time of war and doing suit every forty days at the Court of the Forest, but in these parts history seems to begin with Charles II, who came hunting: many houses claim that he slept there ... Rhinefield is one of these.

By the eighteenth century, Brockenhurst was a cluster of cottages between two big estates, New Park and Brockenhurst Park. In the heyday of smuggling, ponies were loaded with contraband landed at Beaulieu and trained to cross Beaulieu Heath on their own, thus diminishing the risk of smugglers being caught red-handed. They were met at Irons Hill just outside Brockenhurst.

It was the coming of the railway which led to the growth of the village into what seems more like a town today. The sidings were laid out for the trucks bringing stone for the building of Rhinefield House. Many motorists will remember Brockenhurst today merely as the little place where they had to stop and wait while trains crossed the main road, missing the row of shops off to the left, the scatter of thatched cottages which remain and the pleasant outskirts where forest invades village still with streams and lawns. Here you can find St Saviour's, a spacious church in Victorian Gothic built by Mrs Walker-Munro in the 1890s. In a corner behind wrought-iron grilles lie the Walker-Munro memorials. The family had originally intended to build a private chapel for Rhinefield, but the vicar of that time persuaded them to provide the larger church to serve the west side of Brockenhurst; however, by 1903 building was still going on and had so far exceeded the original estimate that no more money was forthcoming. After a temporary wall had been put up across the unfinished west end, the church was finally opened in 1905. Four grandsons of the Walker-Munros put up sufficient money to build the west end, and the church was completed in 1961.

Perhaps the most striking building along the main road is Carey's Manor, its half-timbered gables and tall chimneys sheltering behind a wall of mellow brick. The original house was the home of John Carey, in the 1670s Riding Forester to Charles II, but this house was put up in 1887 and is now a hotel. Built in Tudor Style, it offers four-poster suites, but there is also a brand-new wing in contemporary style to house heated swimming-pool, sauna and gymnasium.

We walked down a lane east of the village and found the north entrance to Brockenhurst Park, an ornate gatehouse with overtones of a castle on the Rhine and swagged with carved garlands, leading to a chestnut avenue. The original house was E-shaped, Queen Anne style, with a round tower. This was bought by the Morant family in 1770 together with four thousand acres of parkland, their home for two centuries, so that the name of Morant crops up frequently in Brockenhurst; the pub by the station is now the Morant Arms, and many cottages around, built for estate workers, have a big black letter M displayed above the front door.

Lady Caroline Morant started a day school for the estate children, presided over by Miss Ash for fifty years. Every Sunday the girls walked to church in straw bonnets accompanied by Miss Ash in her chair drawn by a donkey; once inside, each girl's apron was attached to Miss Ash's by a chain of safety pins so they should kneel upright. For the annual treat held within the park, the children formed a procession with Miss Ash at the head, the donkey on this occasion wearing white cotton drawers tied with the Morant family colours, blue and yellow.

The old manor was pulled down recently and a modern, brick house erected in its place. A watercolour in Horace Hutchinson's book on the forest, published in 1904, shows the gardens at perfection, long yew walks trimmed into arches and walls, fountains playing, a peacock posing on the steps, so when the present-day gardens were opened to the public in the spring of 1984 we had paid them a visit.

On the edge of the gardens, bluebells lay in drifts under the rhododendrons, pink and white ornamental cherries and glossy-leaved magnolias holding up white and crimson blossoms. Further on were the yew walks, clipped to less exuberant shapes than a hundred years ago but still impressive. Down one long aisle of dark hedges we saw an ornate urn on a stone plinth and went respectfully to investigate. The stone said, 'To Fido'.

The formal gardens are laid out in front of the new house, old brick arbours and balustrades, arches and statues and a canal full of lilies contrasting sharply with the dark brick and stark modern lines of the new house which gazes out over all, between huge old cedars and cork oaks, another link with the past.

We had come in a side entrance, not under the gatehouse, and, returning this way along the lane, came to Brockenhurst church, a little way out of the village, set on a wooded mound without a house in sight, long and low with a roof of old tiles, a small brick tower surmounted by a spire topped by a very grand gilt cockbird, the oldest church in the forest as it is now, the only one mentioned in the Domesday Book: 'Broceste, here is a church.' There is even some Saxon masonry in one wall.

Petunias made a bright show against the grey stones of the porch: inside we were confronted with a fine Norman archway over the south door. The gallery still remains across the west end: here the church musicians used to play for the services, accompanying on violins and wind instruments until a harmonium was installed, and later an organ. Round the walls are memorial tablets to the Morant family, patrons of the living, and the royal arms of Queen Anne, in high relief. On either side of the chancel, tall, narrow, thirteenth-century windows are filled with beautiful stained-glass flowers, a vine, lilies, passionflowers and sunflowers. There are some striking modern windows in the newer north aisle, one showing St Francis surrounded by ducklings, a jay, sparrowhawk, partridge and hoopoe.

Outside stands the great yew tree, thought to be the same age as the church, with a girth of more than twenty feet. Old prints show a small thatched shed nearby, where the vicar used to leave his horse during services.

On the north side lies the main burial ground, sloping gently down hill to green fields. The old graves lay bowered in wild flowers, orchids and moon daisies, purple knapweeds, pink willow herb, yellow ladies' bedstraw so that a stone bird perched on a tombstone seemed so natural he might fly away and the grass was all aflicker with butterflies, common blues, meadow browns and burnet moths feeding on birds' foot trefoil, an unexpected sanctuary.

However, the right-hand side was all mown and tidy. Under one imposing cenotaph lie rows of identical white tombstones each planted with heather or roses, red and white, more than a hundred, the graves of New Zealand and other soldiers, victims of Gallipoli who died of their wounds in Carey's Manor and other local houses commandeered as hospitals in the 1914-18 War. Every year a memorial service is held here on the Sunday nearest to Anzac Day.

Nearby is an ornate marble tombstone in memory of Brusher Mills, a strange irony, for the money spent on it, raised by public subscription, would have done Brusher a power of good in his lifetime.

Brusher is said to have acquired his name from his sweeping of the cricket pitch, Brockenhurst being famous for the game: the Morant Arms was formerly called 'The Bat and Ball'. On the other hand, his early life was spent at Foxlease, where he is said to have brushed the frozen lake for skating parties. Whatever the truth, Brusher is chiefly famous for his activities as a snake-catcher. He lived for nearly twenty years in an old charcoal-burner's hut, north of Holland's Wood. With a pair of tongs and a forked stick – and often his bare hands – he caught snakes and kept them in a sack till there was sufficient quantity to put on the train and send to London Zoo, who paid him one shilling each in the 1870s. He was also much in demand as a forest guide, spending his tips at the Railway Inn. At the age of sixty-five he died of a heart attack, alone in an outhouse – the marble tombstone does not mention that. A more fitting memorial stands in Brockenhurst itself, where the Railway Inn has changed its name to 'The Snake-Catcher'.

After Brusher's death the forked stick and long-handled tongs were passed on to George Wateridge, who continued to supply zoos in London and Scotland but did not capture the public imagination like Brusher, perhaps because he lived in a cottage in the normal way. Today of course it is illegal to kill or remove snakes from the forest.

Leaving the church, we went to see a Brockenhurst character very much alive; indeed, quite recently she had begun a new life.

Whenever Greta Hopkinson moved house with her doctor husband, it was she who put up new bookcases, made new cupboards, anything to do with wood. Left a widow, she settled in Brockenhurst and made more cupboards, until by chance going to an exhibition of birds carved from wood. These fired her with the desire to carve, rather than continue with carpentry, so at the age of sixty-eight she enrolled at Lymington Community Centre to learn the use of chisel and goudge.

A friend, hearing of her new obsession, found a chunk of ancient yew wood lying in Lymington car-park, took it to Brockenhurst and threw it over Mrs Hopkinson's gate. This became her first carving, a cloaked woman of sorrow twenty inches tall, the grain and subtle shades of wood heightened by hours of polishing.

'The wood tells you what to do,' she told us, so much of her time has been spent searching for the right pieces. A great knot of roots hauled out of a forest river and brought home in a wheelbarrow weighed ten stone before it dried out.

After housework and gardening – and even then her mind dwells with the piece in hand – Greta Hopkinson's real day starts at tea-time when she retires to her work room. A new sculpture begins with the wood being cleaned up and brooded upon to find what is within it; then it is given shape by trimming off a few inches or sawing out large chunks; when the shape seems right, there come endless hours of polishing every cranny with beeswax to bring out the beauty of the wood itself; in all it may take several months to finish.

The first thing that struck us was Greta Hopkinson's incredible energy, for much of her sculpting involves hard physical labour, moving heavy wood with a pulley, hours of sawing and goudging, and heaving about – she is after all in her eighties. Once in her studio, however, we forgot all that, for the sculptures are so powerful and passionate they make you gasp aloud. That knot of roots is a horrific writhing called 'Snake Pit'; a branch of black bog oak three thousand years old plunges into darkness, 'The Descent of Lucifer'; a serpent opens pale, threatening jaws. But none of these is an ordinary animal carving; the wood speaks for itself. A great grey donkey's head looking over a forked tree appears to become a long-tailed bird with threatening talons when turned round.

Not all emanate darkness: 'Rising Blessing' soars upward; there are birds, ships, flames, but the room is dominated by a life-size figure, wild, tattered and demonic, called 'Dark

Shepherd'. Greta Hopkinson has had four exhibitions of her work, fittingly called 'Dead Wood Alive'. It is a measure of her powerful vision that every walk in the forest since has been enriched for us – every dead branch and trunk must be studied for the message within.

A tributary of the Lymington River runs past the house, and there she finds some of her best wood. The river itself flows across Balmer Lawn, and on a summer Sunday this is one of the most crowded honeypots in the forest with car-parking beside it, grassy banks and water usually just deep enough for children to play and adults to swim.

People of all ages clad in anything from lounge suit to briefest bikini were strolling, reading, sleeping, shouting at kids, staring into space or licking ice-creams from the van parked nearby, the grass strewn with rugs, chairs, balls, magazines in bright primary colours. In the river two men raced each other to the road bridge, free style between children paddling rubber dinghies, red, blue and orange and wading mums seeing fair play. Two black labradors paddled together in quiet dignity, occasionally exchanging a gruff word like elderly clubmen. On the far bank two impromptu cricket matches were being played oblivious of traffic, roaring past in a constant stream over the bridge.

Beyond Balmer Lawn Hotel a proper match was in progress on Brusher's old pitch. The big hotel building was marshalling headquarters for the invasion of Normandy when a stupendous number of troops had to be brought south, in complete secrecy and concentrated along the south coast ready for D-Day. Intelligence designed a signboard to hang outside the hotel bearing a code message for what was going on. It showed a mother duck with outspread wings urging her ducklings into the water.

Balmer Lawn itself is a vast stretch of grass where the pony races used to be held – now ponies only graze upon it. We decided to picnic there in the shade of a vast oak, disturbing first of all a young adder of the brick red colour Dickie had described as 'jumping up at you' – however, this one slipped quickly away into the bracken – and then a much larger grass snake. Now and then horse-drawn wagons passed by on a gravel track leading into the forest, so we went to visit their owner.

New Forest Wagons started up in 1975 with permission to use forestry tracks forbidden to the car, so it is a lovely quiet, relaxed way to enjoy the woods. The horses, of which there are ten, are Percherons, Shires and Clydesdales, all saved from slaughter because they can still cope with the gentle forest ambles. Our wagon was drawn by Monty, a bay Shire with enormous shaggy fetlocks. He had previously been employed by a London company who run horse-drawn buses for tourists. On the wagon we sat back to back facing outward as in an Irish jaunting-car and set out up the track, Tilery Road, soon passing the site of the Victoria Brick and Tile Works.

The wagons creak along at walking pace and we are free to gaze out at the passing forest, a wide driftway left unplanted where ponies graze, a plantation of Douglas fir all dark and bare floored, then a patch of oaks wide spread with new bracken beneath and little second-bloom foxgloves sprouting from main stems. Passing a big wood ants' nest under some spruce, we came to a clearing recently felled. Douglas fir was stacked all along the track trimmed and ready for loading, filling the air with its smell. Deer fence, six foot tall, surrounded a newly planted stretch though rosebay willow herb and self-sown birch hid – and protected – the infant trees.

We had circled Pignall and Stubby Copse and were passing through a mixed wood of wide-spaced oak and beech when we glimpsed a single red deer. Gatekeeper butterflies and meadow browns sunned themselves on bramble flowers by the track but no birds sang, only a jay scolded from a high branch. Monty brought us back to Standing Hat and we said goodbye to him with regret. He wore pink net caps trimmed with bobbles over his ears, to keep the flies out.

Wagon rides can be booked in advance from the gift shop in Balmer Lawn Road: even dogs can go if well behaved.

To search out Wahlenbergia though, it was necessary to go on foot, even on all fours at times.

Ivy-leaved bellflower likes damp woodland edges. We had found it some years ago in the heart of the forest and went to

Woodland Creatures: Red deer calf

Grey squirrel

Young fox

Grass snake

Fallow fawn

Badger foraging at night

visit the place again, hoping the little flower had survived – in fact, to our delight it had increased. A small bog slopes down to a runnel, sheltered on three sides by spinneys and bright with spearwort, a secret place. A grass snake which had just shed its skin, showing off the bright yellow collar, was gliding through tufts of sphagnum searching for water – some of the bog mosses had turned papery grey in the drought. Following the snake downhill, we found water still flowing in the runnel and all along its moist banks the delicate pale blue of ivy-leaved bellflower starring the grass, growing thick enough to haze the bank in places with its lilac-blue. Though here it had spread to a streamside across the path, ivy-leaved bellflower is very uncommon now, extinct in the Isle of Wight, a tiny forest gem to be cherished.

New Park Manor also claims to be in the heart of the forest, and it is splendidly situated for exploring the whole area, just north of Brockenhurst down a long drive winding through parkland which once a year becomes the focus of traffic from far and near on the days of the New Forest Show, at the end of July.

New Park was an ancient hunting lodge, new in 1484 when John Hoton was living there, in contrast to Old Park at Lyndhurst which was established in 1291. But it was in 1660 that New Park really came into its own with the Restoration of Charles II, when it became his favourite hunting lodge in the forest. The land was already 'divided with pales, lodges and ditches into several meadows and pastures, four hundred and ninety eight timber trees and beech trees, stocked with cattle and horses'. The King 'enclosed with pales certain lands adjoining for the preservation of our red deer, newly come out of France'.

However, the King's mind was not entirely on hunting, since Nell Gwynn accompanied him to New Park on some visits. Moreover, Winifred Wells, a lady of his court, was given all the timber in three nearby woods, New Copse, Irons Hill and King's Copse – the King would have given her more had not the Lord Treasurer intervened!

During his reign nearly three hundred trees were sent from New Park to build ships for the Navy.

Pigs at pannage

William Cobbett, in the early nineteenth century, had enthusiastic plans for planting locust trees to provide more timber for the dockyards. He found the trees during an American tour and was so sure of their future value to English forests that he started a nursery on Long Island, raising thousands of them from seed, to send home. Three years later he came to New Park to see the Commissioner of Woods and Forests and also to inspect the plantation of locust trees. 'There is a garden, a farmyard, a farm and a nursery. The place looks like a considerable gentleman's seat, the house stands in a sort of park and you can see a great deal of expense has been incurred in levelling the ground and making it pleasing to the eye of my lords, the Commissioners.' He went on to make scathing remarks about the expense of keeping the forest just for the deer and demanded to know just how many the royal family actually ate, per year! The locust trees disappointed him too – indeed, they never took on as timber trees here since they tend to grow crooked.

New Park was later home to the Deputy Surveyor of the New Forest but is now a hotel with its own riding-stables, its fields the site of many shows and gymkhanas.

The oldest part of the house, dating from the very founding of the New Forest, is some eleventh-century ships' timbers forming part of the floor. The Victorians, disliking rough beams, covered the Tudor work with carved panels on the ground and first floor. To make a very comfortable modern hotel the house has been much altered to include many bathrooms, central heating, bars and so on. To find history we had to go upstairs to the second floor. This is where the maids lived, and so this part was left alone by the Victorians. Here are sloping ceilings, and black Tudor beams outcropping from the walls. Here the knocker-up went along every morning, waking the staff, and you can hear his ghost daily at 4.30 a.m., thumping the doors, we were told.

On the first floor King Charles' bedroom stretches half the width of the house, with four windows overlooking the gardens, each with a stained-glass design incorporating pomegranates, from the royal arms of his wife, Catherine of Braganza. All the door handles are stylized brass acorns, celebrating the King's hiding place in an oak tree on his escaping to France in 1651. As you would expect, the ghost of Nell Gwynn often glides down to the river to bathe …

Between events the show grounds are quiet pasture, and it would rejoice King Charles II's heart to see the herd of seventy to eighty fallow deer which often come in to take advantage of the good grazing, though they move out in July when all the marquees and caravans begin to move in for The Show.

Many displays and events have their counterpart in shows all over England, but some are special to the New Forest, such as the Woodmen's competitions where the aim is to turn out the maximum number of fencing stakes from one length of timber in seventy-five minutes, Hampshire blacksmiths and farriers demonstrating horse-shoeing, and the driving classes which included four-in-hand, donkey driving and heavy horse turnouts. In the wide green setting of New Park show rings, broken here and there by giant oaks, we particularly enjoyed the parade of light trade turnouts, milk floats, butchers' traps, market carts, a fishmonger and poulterer's cart and London trolleys all smartly turned out, each drawn by a single horse impeccably groomed, its driver dressed according to trade, the butchers for example in straw boaters and striped aprons.

In the New Forest Exhibition tent various organizations such as Hampshire and Isle of Wight Naturalists Trust and the New Forest Association had displays of information, posters and tea towels for sale, and stewards to answer questions and enrol new members. One stand was called 'Help us build the New Forest Centre', the aim being to raise half a million pounds to build a centre and museum on a site in Lyndhurst car-park.

The Forestry Commission showed an exhibition of photographs and outdoors a cool woodland walk into the forest itself with labelled trees. The sun shone brilliantly over New Park, and we were glad to sink down on a shady seat – to find ourselves staring at the stump of a recently felled tree: it was a locust, surely a descendant of Cobbett's plantations? Today they are usually called false acacia and much planted as ornamental trees in parks; closely related to the laburnum, it bears white drooping chains of flowers.

Before leaving the New Park area, we went to visit the Buckhound Kennels in the grounds, founded by Charles II. With the passing of the Deer Removal Act in 1851, the Royal Buckhounds took their toll and were then disbanded. Deer were indiscriminately killed and persecuted till the forest was said to be cleared, but as we have seen, small herds survived and these were hunted by a pack called the New Forest Deerhounds from Wilverley, then later from Hinchelsea. By 1901 O.T. Price of New Park was Master, and it was he who moved the kennels back to the grounds; new buildings were put up in 1911. In 1942 most of the pack had to be put down through wartime shortages, only 2½ couples being left, but even by 1944 efforts were being made to get them going again. In 1950 Sir Dudley Forwood, whom we had met at Old House, became Master, and the pack began once more to flourish.

The hounds crowded to the wire of their enclosure to sniff at us, big brown, black and white dogs, alert and friendly, bred in the kennels. A nursing bitch allowed us to see her exceptionally large litter of nine fat, nuzzling puppies. As hunting, for fallow buck only, is from August to April, this was a rest month. The pack had been out for a two-hour run that morning, just for exercise, and would have another that evening with perhaps a swim in the river. They hunt in season twice a week, killing one buck out of four or five hunted, averaging about ten kills in a season – the antlers of last season's kill were ranged round the stable. Much of their work involved merely moving a herd, splitting it up or driving it off private ground.

Asked what defence she would make against accusations of cruelty, the Joint Master said, 'This is the cleanest form of hunting. First of all we single out a buck which is less than perfect, to retain good breeding stock. As to the actual kill, when a deer seeks cover, he lies down and the hounds come up and bay. At once the hunt servants go in and kill with a humane killer.' Afterwards, the body is gralloched that is, disembowelled, and the hounds are allowed to eat the entrails, certainly a bloody sight. Misunderstood glimpses of this brought down wild accusations of deer being torn to pieces, the Master said. New Forest Buckhounds are thought to be the only pack in the world hunting fallow buck.

Coming from New Park back onto the hot and noisy main road, it was a relief to take to the woods again, opposite Balmer Lawn. For anyone who wants to venture deeper than waymarked paths but is not entirely sure of his map-reading, one of the pleasantest ways of exploring is simply to follow a river – you will need boots.

We set out to walk up Highland Water under the shade of beech and oak. Here the river has carved an intricate geography of twists and turns, little islands, foot-wide backwaters and shingly beaches. One of the runnels we had to wade through was seething with hundreds of tiny silvery fish. Soon all is quiet but for the river's rippling round a sharp bend. A wren swept across our path to alight in a holly bush, tail up straight with indignation, scolding us sharply and he no bigger than an oak leaf. Wood pigeons also took exception to our presence, flying up from the canopy and clapping their wings.

Presently we sat down on the bank where an oak had crashed down and made a natural bridge across, with a view downstream of green leaves reflected in the river, and water light playing on the boles of beeches. A grey squirrel appeared on the opposite bank, ran out onto a crescent of shingle, leaned forward and drank with small, careful sips, and quite close a cuckoo called, though his voice should have broken by now.

In Queen Bower some of the huge old spreading oaks bear a yellow flash which means they are genetically sound – their acorns will be specially gathered and sent to the nurseries. Queens Beech, silvery barked and immensely tall, has a trunk the size of four normal beeches pillared together, some four hundred years old. A flash of brilliant blue, tantalizingly swift, and a kingfisher has flashed up the river and out of sight: the banks are high here, providing good nesting holes.

Trees fell away on our right. Queen Mead is a vast field where deer are said to gather. We had never found any here, but climbed up to the observation platform for which we had a key. Only Hereford cattle are in sight.

Here and there a tree had fallen, leaving a gap in the canopy through which the sun shone. In each such clearing, bramble bushes had sprung up and now in pink flower afforded food for butterflies otherwise in short supply. One bush was all aflicker with silver-washed fritillaries, orange with black markings, gatekeepers and even a white admiral. Should more be done to encourage bramble and so increase our diminishing butterfly population?

Crashings in the undergrowth heralded only three brown cattle in search of a drink in the river. Male fern and hart's tongue grow along the banks, fragrant meadowsweet and honeysuckle where enough light filters through. Where the river has carved small bays and the water is almost still, dragon and damsel flies hover, emerald green, banded gold and black or metallic blue. As we come into Brinken Wood, where birch, beech and oak are widely spaced with green lawns between, we hardly bother to glance up at one more crashing in the bushes, but we do, just in time. For it is a roe deer, a buck, goat size in fine foxy red summer coat and small, sharp antlers; he bounds away at sight of us with a flash of pale rump.

Roe are smaller than fallow, with a brighter summer coat. They tend to move about for most of the year in family groups rather than herds: the roe family resembles the average human one, mother, father and two young ones. Mating is usually in July or August – this one we thought had probably recently mated as afterwards the bucks wander off on their own for a time, shedding their antlers late in the year and growing their winter coats, usually a darker grey brown. Though the female mates in summer, the foetus does not begin to grow until December, so the fawns, usually twins, are born in May or June with rich brown, white-speckled fur, spending much of their time lying up in sheltering undergrowth while the mother moves off to graze.

We were specially pleased with this deer sighting because roe are notoriously shy, hiding away in thickets or dense forest by day and coming out to feed mostly at night. A gentle, secret creature then – except in the mating season; then the bucks become fiercely possessive of their females and their territory. Though their antlers are far less impressive than a fallow's, they are dagger sharp so that bucks have been known to kill each other in a fight.

Walking on through Brinken Wood, we came to a trodden-down circle of ground, the trees round it with wounded bark and torn branches, a rutting ring. The buck has a gland on his forehead which secretes a scent for marking the boundary of his territory – he may even attack a human who trespasses inside it! All this churning up of the woodland floor was done by his chasing the doe around.

Roe deer are natives of Britain, though they seemed to die out for a time in southern England. In 1800 Lord Dorchester brought some roe to his estate at Milton Abbas in Dorset to provide hunting for the local buckhounds. Over the years they escaped and spread eastward, reaching the New Forest by the 1870s, where they have thriven in its acres of secret covert.

Turning off through a close plantation of oak and beech a mere thirty years old, we came presently to a narrow road. If we turned down it, we should come to a handful of houses by the main road, called Bank, though the name on old maps is Annis Bank. The big house, Annesley, obviously takes its name from that: it was built by the Maxwells.

In 1861 John Maxwell was struggling to launch a new magazine to be called *Robin Goodfellow*. Serial stories were all the rage at that time: he had seen some promising work by a young writer, Mary Braddon, and asked her to write a serial. Mary, who was twenty-four, had enjoyed only limited success so far: for *Robin Goodfellow* she wrote *Lady Audley's Secret*, which sold all over the world, eventually reaching a million copies.

Mary afterwards married John Maxwell, continuing to write under the name of Braddon. One of her novels is called *Mount Royal*, the old name of Northerwood House. The Maxwells lived partly at Bank, partly in Richmond, but in either house Mary wrote on, though none of her later stories ever achieved the fame of *Lady Audley's Secret*, which was praised by such eminent writers as Thackeray and Stevenson. When *The Green Curtain* was published in 1911, it was her eightieth, and last, novel.

Annesley was more recently bought by Dr Barnardo's for use as a home but is now flats.

However, we turned up the narrow road to Gritnam, a hamlet right in the forest, seldom found by visitors, yet with an entry in the Domesday Book, its name deriving from Greatham (three different spellings are correct here), the great homestead. 'Bolle lives in Gretenham. He has half a hide from the King. It was held by Warleran the Huntsman. It is now in the forest. It was worth forty shillings.' A hide varied in actual size according to its fertility; it meant enough land to support one household.

Today there are half a dozen cottages largely for forestry workers, in a clearing surrounded by little lawns, streams, thickets and wood in all its manifestations, wooden fences round all the gardens, logs in great piles already seasoning for winter, a green woodpecker tapping away at a dead oak and a grove of alder buckthorn which used to be a favourite wood for producing charcoal.

Everyone must be out at work for only red admirals and tortoiseshell butterflies move in the bright gardens, and a stock dove croons from the encircling forest.

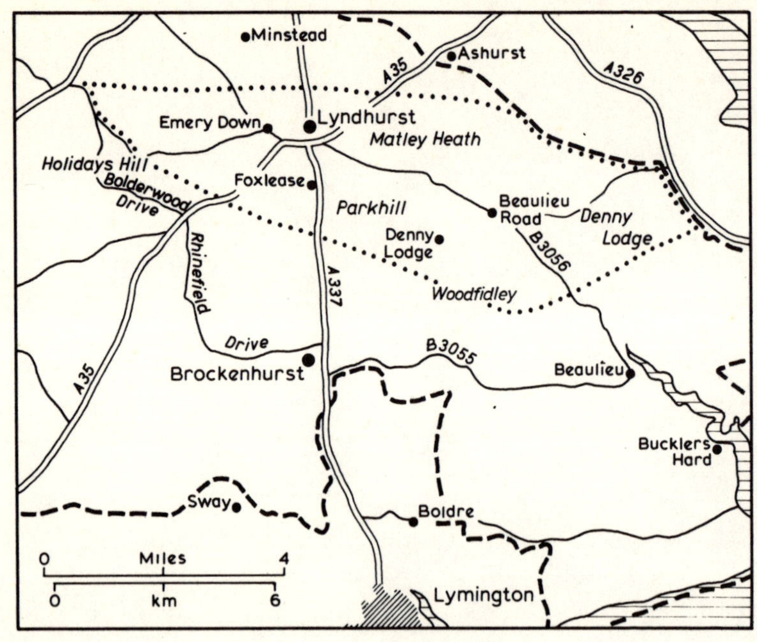

Lyndhurst and Eastwards

6 *Lyndhurst and Eastwards*

Seeing the caravans scattered about among birch and beech, you might think Holidays Hill aptly named – it is one of the smaller camp sites, but the name was originally Halliday's Hill. There is a forest lodge tucked away down a long gravel track, in front of it a spread of heath and birch where fallow deer steal out at dusk, behind it the Reptiliary.

This was set up by the Forestry Commission to educate the public, encouraging visitors to appreciate the beauty and interest of these largely unloved creatures – often grass snakes are killed because they are mistaken for adders. The Reptiliary's other function is to breed the rarer species such as the sand lizard to enlarge the number in the wild.

In a clearing stand a number of pits with concrete walls and nets over the top. We did not stop this time at the adder or grass snake pits, having seen both frequently in the forest, but went straight to the smooth snake: these are very rare now and we had not seen one this year. Each pit contains the kind of terrain which the reptile would choose – the grass snakes' includes a pond large enough for them to swim in. The smooth snakes have a hillock of heather, gorse and birch scrub: at first all seems motionless, then with a faint rustle of dead leaves one appears, gliding along right below the wall, very slim with a pronounced neck and silvery grey body.

Smooth snakes were first discovered near Bournemouth in 1859: today they are found occasionally in Dorset and Surrey as well as the New Forest; they are harmless and protected not only by forest bye-laws but also by the 1975 Conservation of Wild Creatures Act. The neighbouring sand lizards are similarly protected. These are also very rare. When myxomatosis destroyed a large number of the rabbit population, the lizards lacked the loose sandy soil round the warrens which they need for breeding, eggs being laid in the sand and hatched by the warmth of the sun. Forest fires and heath burning have also taken their toll. But here in their pit they were darting about, handsome yellow-brown little creatures dappled with darker markings, and one male with green flanks.

Further pits held common lizards and slow worms together, others with large ponds and tall reed mace houses newts, toads and frogs. All three kinds of newt, the smooth, palmate and crested, can be found in forest ponds, though they hibernate on land. While they may account for a few toads' eggs in spring, newt co-habits peacefully enough in the pit with its toad companions.

When the Reptiliary was first set up, the snakes were housed together, but it was discovered, surprisingly, that the harmless and slender smooth snakes were eating the adders!

Grown-up families of house martens flickered round the roof of the keeper's lodge, and from logs already piled for winter came a delicate high sound like the whirring of a tiny sewing-machine – a wood cricket. Tall old beeches hide the river below, their foliage tired and shabby now and almost hidden by their rich crop of mast, so thick it turns each tree brown – the pigs will do well this year. A grove of crab apples is similarly covered with fruit, a blackbird already busy on the fallers beneath.

We could walk down Highland Water to the Bournemouth road, or over Roman Arch, a small brick bridge spanning the river, marking the course of the old route from Lyndhurst to Christchurch, but instead we strike northward through a magnificent wood of Douglas fir, their purple-brown trunks soaring to a hundred feet: these were planted in 1925 and later thinned so that each tree could grow to its maximum size – a conifer wood at its best with enough sunlight not only to disperse the usual gloom but to encourage the natural regenerations of the trees. Here were infant Lawson cypress, larch and of course Douglas fir, albeit only one foot tall.

On our right a deer fence protected a new planting. Bracken and birch had already sprung up almost hiding – and therefore protecting – the young trees: they looked like Christmas trees but were in fact yet one more stage of Douglas fir. Along the path grew a few Scots pine with their orange-brown trunks, and sitka spruce, easy to recognize from its bark which grows in small, round plates. Very quiet, only magpies scolding somewhere and a nuthatch tip-tapping, until we reach a gate onto the road from Lyndhurst to Ringwood which comes up from Emery Down, one of the most delightful roads in the forest, passing through ancient woods and open heathlands, well furnished with hidden car-parks and picnic places and walkers' tracks.

We turned westwards as far as Mogshade Hill, a mere 340 feet high but a splendid viewpoint. While the month of August means dusty needles and shabby leaves in the woods, here on the open heathland the heather comes into its full glory, spreading away, hazing the land with purple all around us. South-westward the heath slopes down to the valley of Bratley Water, while beyond the woods rise up, dark against a sunset sky, Bratley, Backley, Oakley, Slufters, Milkham.

Behind us, by the road, stands a tall wooden cross, backed by the pines of Highland Water Inclosure. Beside it stand two flagpoles and several young maples. The inscription reads, 'On this site a cross was erected to the glory of God on 14th April 1944. Services were held here until D. Day, 6th of June 1944 by men of the 3rd Canadian Division R.C.A.S.C.' A memorial service is held here every year.

You would not expect, driving along a wooded road, to come across a large stone fireplace, by itself, with no dwelling in sight, but there it is on our right as we walk back towards Lyndhurst, a stone hearth and massive three-tiered chimney rising some ten feet from a grassy picnic area, a reminder this time of an earlier war. It is inscribed, 'This is the site of a hutted camp occupied by a Portuguese Army Unit during the First World War. This unit assisted the depleted local labour force in producing timber for the war effort. The Forestry Commission have retained this fireplace from the cookhouse as a memorial to the men who lived and worked here.'

Close by there are picnic tables and another kind of fireplace, a permanent barbecue, for which you need a permit from the Forestry Commission. Birch and pine enclose a semicircle of grass; a bed of bog myrtle encircles each solitary birch as if planted – a lovely spot for an evening party. On this visit we found the air rich with smells from the barbecue, onion, sausage and woodsmoke, while alfresco badminton went on across the grass. From here you can take our track through the Douglas firs to Holiday Hill and return along the bank of Highland Water or cross the road to Millyford Bottom and follow the river in its upper reaches.

It was a Saturday afternoon when we came to Swan Green, on the western outskirts of Lyndhurst now but once a hamlet on its own. Here was the kind of 'Summer in Britain' picture we like to present to overseas visitors, a sloping green surrounded on two sides by woodland, on the others by whitewashed thatched cottages – and on the green a game of cricket in progress, two white figures making runs, a scatter of applause. There are several huge old oaks and beeches, outliers of Lyndhurst Wood, actually on the pitch, so the ball disappears into their foliage from time to time, before plopping back onto the grass. Small boys prefer to play football, just inside the boundary, and the Bournemouth traffic speeds by the southern end unheeded. When the match is over, players can adjourn to the Swan Inn.

Some of the cottages were built for servants at Northerwood House, the 'big house' close by, reached by a drive winding through rhododendrons. It was called Northerwood in 1741, then changed its name for a time to Mount Royal. When it was owned by Lord Londesborough, he decided to start a cricket team and had the present pitch laid out on Swan Green. When Northerwood was owned by the Bowes-Lyons, the Queen Mother's family, a piper used to parade up and down the terrace every night after dinner; on a still night the bagpipes could be plainly heard in Lyndhurst High Street.

In 1945 it was presented to the Forestry Commission and used by them as a training centre – old students still remember the delicious food! Today it is let into flats, and some of the grounds are built over, but the gardens remain, a terrace with wide views to the south and over the village, together with some fine old trees – beech, sweet gum and cypress among them.

Just north of Swan Green lies Emery Down, a little village mentioned in 1379 as Emerichdon, a mixture today of old brick cottages, new bungalows and some picturesque almshouses built round a courtyard; hidden away up among the beech woods' edges are more opulent houses standing in their own grounds, a Mercedes or Aston Martin in the drive. One lane, Silver Street, is named from *silva*, meaning woodland. The village school building now houses the Office of the Verderers, guardians of the forest bye-laws, in the village where squatters would once run up a cabin overnight on land poached from the forest.

In 1863 Admiral Frederick Boultbee retired to live in Emery Down in a thatched cottage which had some time previously been the village inn, then called the Running Horse. Deciding that the place needed a church, he was granted a plot of Crown land on the west side of the street and there erected a brick church, opened in 1864. He also built and endowed the alms houses: his cottage is now the vicarage.

Uriah Lawrence had paid 4½d a year rates for the Running Horse; then the village was left without a pub. The Office of Woods, predecessors of the Forestry Commission, became very worried in the later eighteenth century about the amount of forest land being encroached for gardens and dwellings: it gave instructions for a detailed map to be prepared showing exactly how much land had been lost in this way. In 1801 a special inquiry was held at the Verderers' Hall, in which Thomas Walton was accused of having a cottage on wheels and twenty lugs of land on Lyndhurst Hill. Thomas was told that this constituted encroachment and he must therefore take the fences down and return the land to the forest.

So what was this cottage on wheels? The men of Emery Down, deprived of their pub, had to look elsewhere for their drink. An arrangement was made for a barrel of mead or ale to be brought up on a dray and parked in the village street; in wet weather this proved a bleak meeting place so the dray was roofed over, then sides were put to it so that it became 'a cottage on wheels', or caravan – which you can still see today.

For never mind what the Verderers Court had ordered, the caravan eventually grew into a pub, the New Forest Inn, beside the mainroad westward, or Saltway as it was called, since the road through Bolderwood was still a mere forest track. Today the New Forest Inn is a large pub divided into snug, low-ceilinged bars, dim lights gleaming on dark beams and horse brasses, with a nice line in hot snacks – and as you come through the front door, you enter the caravan, its wooden shape still preserved as a kind of entrance hall, though it is not 'a cottage on wheels' anymore.

Walking back through Swan Green towards Lyndhurst, we pass the great trees of Cuffnell's. Here stood a Georgian mansion owned in 1784 by Sir George Rose, later Deputy Warden of the New Forest, a well-known political figure of the times who frequently entertained George III and Queen Charlotte on their journeys to and from Weymouth. However, it was chiefly famous as the home of 'Alice in Wonderland', after she had married and become Alice Hargreaves. Later the house became a hotel, then during the last war the headquarters for a searchlight battery. Afterwards it was demolished, the Alice in Wonderland murals came crashing down, and now only the trees remain to evoke the White Rabbit, the Cheshire Cat.

Lyndhurst, named after the lime or linden tree, was already a royal manor in the tenth century, being given to the Abbey of Amesbury. In the Domesday survey we read, 'The King holds Lyndhurst. It was assessed at two hides. Herbert the Forester now holds one virgate' (about thirty acres). Even then the manor had an important position for it was a crossroads of forest tracks connecting Southampton and Lymington, Beaulieu and Christchurch, Winchester and Ringwood and many smaller settlements.

One of the oldest things in Lyndhurst must be Park Pale, a bank encircling the original Deer Park, which we went to see last winter. They were felling hardwoods in Park Hill: a great beech fell with a noise like thunder, shaking the ground before the wood sank back into its winter silence. To reach Park Pale we had to walk down a straight gravel track lined on both sides as far as the eye could see, with stacks of wood, and all of it set up by one man.

This was wood assigned to properties still holding the right of estover, that is to have fuel from the forest. The wood is cut and

Secret Forest: Wild gladiolus

Flies feeding on stinkhorn fungus

Bark carving on Woodfidley beech

Water violets

Foxgloves

Marsh gentian

Male fern flourishing in a moist glade

stacked into cords, each eight feet long, four feet high and four feet wide. The owners will be told where their 'sign-wood' is, then they must arrange to cart it away. Beyond the stacks of logs we found the bank of Park Pale, which seemed quite small in comparison, eroded away over the centuries from when it was first thrown up in 1291. Like the specimen inclosure bank we had seen at Rhinefield, it would have had a wooden paling fence along the top.

The most historic building in Lyndhurst is of course Queens House – a much older one must once have stood on the site, for Lyndhurst has always been the capital of the New Forest. As early as 1279 a demand went out for 'twenty oaks to make laths for the use of the Queen's manor house'. The house continued to be enlarged and repaired over the years until in the seventeenth century it was rebuilt, on the orders of Charles I, who ordered, 'a new building of divers lodgings for our use and service adjoining to the old house at Lyndhurst, as also a kitchyn, pantrie, larder and other offices and a stable to contain fortie horse'. The King was never to see his new manor, but the rebuilding was completed by Charles II, 250 loads of timber having been sold to finance it.

Charles II and James II hunted from Lyndhurst. George III was the last monarch to stay here, the village people being allowed to peer in through the windows to watch him eating! The house became the residence of the Warden of the Forest, then of the Deputy Surveyor, who had previously lived at New Park. When that great character Gerald Lascelles held the office, he kept his trained falcons here and regularly rode the forest with one set upon his wrist.

Today, after several more restorations, Queens House dominates the western approach to Lyndhurst, a massive brick mansion showing its seventeenth-century face to the road with tall, Tudor-style chimneys and the four distinctive pointed dormers of its second storey. It is now headquarters of the Forestry Commission in the south-east – except for the Verderers' Hall, originally a separate building at the eastern end.

The Normans brought their language with them so that the green forest became the vert, and the officers appointed to look after it the Verderers. In the eighteenth century, when kings lost interest in hunting in the New Forest, justice declined also, so the Verderers were given powers to fine or imprison for the breaking of forest laws. For many years a condition of taking office was the ownership of seventy-five acres of land with common rights, but this was all changed by the New Forest Act of 1949, which reduced the qualifying acreage to one. There are ten Verderers now, five nominated by various bodies such as the Countryside Commission, and five elected by the commoners, since much of the Verderers' work is concerned with the welfare of animals depastured on the forest.

The Verderers' Court, held six times yearly, is open to the public, so we went to the July session. The court is an austere building even though the walls are at present painted coral pink. The main seating is a central block of open-backed wooden pews facing raised benches for the Verderers and the old prisoners' dock made of rough-hewn oak. Above the oak panelling of the lower walls are mounted various antlers and a reproduction of the New Forest Embroidery. Black beams, paved floor and stained-glass windows all give off an atmosphere of ancient tradition, as did the opening proceedings.

The Agisters in their green coats were grouped at the side of the dock. The senior Agister stood up, raised his right hand and proclaimed, 'Oyez, oyez, oyez! All manner of persons who have any presentment or matter or thing to do at this Court of Swainmote let him come forward and he shall be heard. God save the Queen.' Anyone might then stand on the dais and state their case.

Matters that day concerned the ownership of some land for sale on the forest border and the number of animals killed on forest roads, nine deer in May and June, and twenty-three ponies, many of them run down, surprisingly, by local motorists, bringing home the necessity of the bye-laws prohibiting the feeding of ponies. We have often seen well-meaning visitors petting ponies at car-parks, not realizing they were encouraging them to seek out dangerous roadsides. We come out of the Verderers' Court into the twentieth-century roar of traffic belting down Lyndhurst High Street and screeching to a halt at the traffic lights. Several routes for a bypass are under debate, all of them fiercely contested as bound to take a swathe out of the forest, so for the present traffic continues to grind round the one-way system.

One of its redeeming features for the motorist is the vast car-park just behind the shops. Here, on a piece of waste land is to be built the New Forest Centre.

After the visit of the Queen and Prince Philip to celebrate nine hundred years of New Forest history, a trust was set up to fund a centre. The plans show a range of elegant timber buildings round a central courtyard, the entrance below the kind of clocktower seen over manor stables. This will house a forest museum, a blacksmith's forge and other craft workshops and a library to which have been donated the papers of the Hon. Gerald Lascelles, that distinguished Deputy Surveyor. The building will also incorporate the information bureau for visitors at present housed temporarily in the car-park.

As part of the same celebrations, the President of the New Forest Society had the brilliant idea of commissioning a tapestry. Local industry donated sufficient funds, and Belinda Montagu designed a history of forest life in three panels to hang between the windows of the Verderers' Court. However, when it was finished, the tapestry was thought to be too valuable to be housed in a building open to the public and unsupervised, so it will eventually find its proper place in the New Forest Centre. For the time being, it hangs in the Council Chamber at Appletree Court.

The photograph on canvas in the Verderers' Hall gives some idea of the tapestry's subtle woodland colouring but loses much of the exquisite detail of the original, which is canvas work and collage. Here is a whole history of the forest glimpsed between trees in foliage of all seasons.

The first panel has Rufus falling from his horse and King John handing a model of Beaulieu Abbey to a monk. The second shows Perkin Warbeck riding to Beaulieu to seek sanctuary after the failure of his rebellion; Margaret Dore, a well-known Beaulieu witch in the eighteenth century, leans upon her stick as a ship is being built at Bucklers Hard. A Scots pine appears for the first time among the oaks and beeches, the first having been planted at Ocknell in 1776. The third panel begins with the first railway, a tall-chimneyed engine steaming between the trunks for the first time in 1847. This is followed by the Hon. Gerald Lascelles, hawk on wrist, Rhinefield House, Brusher Mills and Alice in Wonderland. A Spitfire fighter, developed in Southampton, then flies overhead. The last part of the panel comes slap up to date with Fawley Oil Refinery chimneys on the skyline, tents and caravans beneath the trees and lastly the Queen planting a commemorative oak sapling.

All among the branches in every panel nest the coats of arms of families connected with the forest; in the first panel four of these recall the queens who once owned Lyndhurst, Eleanor of Castile, Margaret of France, Isabella of France and Philippa of Hainault.

But what give the tapestry its unique New Forest atmosphere are all the creatures who creep, fly or gallop across it and the variety of fern and flower all realized in brilliant detail, a brimstone butterfly with its red spots, a sinuously patterned grass snake, a gorse bush where a silver-studded blue butterfly is feeding while Dartford warblers perch on the top – the New Forest Centre will be worth a visit for the tapestry alone, though its other treasures will be much appreciated considering there has been no museum until now devoted to the forest.

Just above the figure of Alice, in the tapestry, stands Lyndhurst parish church, built in 1863. The real building curiously patterned in red and yellow brick stands on a hillock near Queens House, its 160-foot spire dominating the village and visible from many places in the forest, a useful landmark. It is thought that a church has stood on this mound for hundreds of years. One was built by George II in 1741, and much frequented by the local gentry hoping to glimpse visiting royalty from the Kings House next door, half a dozen opulent carriages waiting outside on a Sunday morning: a mere fifty years after its building, the plain, galleried church was said to be too small.

Eventually the old church was pulled down and the present one built, completed by the spire in 1868. A door at the west end admits royalty from Queens House – we enter from the north.

Clerestory windows makes it so light one is immediately struck by the wealth of decoration and colour which lend it almost the feeling of an Eastern church. This is partly the effect of the walls themselves, geometrically patterned in red, white and yellow local bricks.

Since the church is dedicated to St Michael and all Angels, there *are* angels, beautifully carved from wood, perched above pillars playing violins and other instruments, while stone ones appear on the pulpit. Lord Leighton's fresco, with life-size figures of the Wise and Foolish Virgins, dominates the east end. Frederick Leighton, as he was then, offered to paint the fresco in 1862 while staying close by. There are several richly carved screens and a fine Flaxman wall tablet of a weeping woman, once part of the Georgian church. More angels look down from the windows. The tall east window and that in the south transept are by Edward Burne Jones, one of the Pre-Raphaelite Brotherhood which included Holman Hunt and Dante Gabriel Rossetti – the latter designed two of the angels above the Answers to Prayer window.

Opinions have always been fiercely divided over the aesthetic value of this brick church, which make it the more interesting to visit: one needs quite a long time to explore all the details of its spacious interior.

Opposite St Michael's stands the church school, a homely looking building put up in 1848. Nevertheless, discipline could be harsh. In 1866 R.A. was punished for playing truant and threatened with fifty lashes if he did it again. This was particularly hard because children were often kept at home by their parents to help with seasonal work. In the school logbook there are references to bark-scraping, collecting wood for baking, potato-picking, hay-making and turf-gathering, though there is also a reference, several years running, to poor attendance because of races on the racecourse. (When the circus came, though, the whole school was given a half holiday.) The racecourse was on the north side of the village beyond Custards – said to be so called from the orchards of custard apples which grew there.

From school and church the main street points eastward, lined with shops (one of them a butcher's famous for its venison), emerging at the far end to a parting of ways and between them the sudden high grassy mound of Bolton's Bench. From the bench itself, which surrounds a clump of yew, we could see westward right across Lyndhurst to Northerwood and east to Southampton Water's chimneys.

South of the village stands a house famous all over the world, Foxlease.

The first mention of a house here was in 1604, when Coxlease is noted as part of Lyndhurst manor lands. It was then a forest keeper's lodge. After the Restoration of Charles II, Mabel Cole petitioned the King for the lease of Coxlease, as a reward for her having looked after Charles I while he was imprisoned in Carisbrooke Castle. By 1770 the house, now known as Foxlease, belonged to Sir Philip Jennings-Clark, a friend of Horace Walpole who had employed the famous Adam brothers to design his villa at Strawberry Hill.

So Sir Philip had an elegant Georgian front built over the Tudor cottage and added an Adam-style drawing-room, among others. Various later tenants made minor alterations, including Mrs Archbold Saunderson, who added a nursery wing but then went to live in the USA, leaving the house empty. When she heard that the Girl Guide movement were interested in Foxlease as a training centre, she gave it to them in honour of the marriage of the Guides' President, Princess Mary, who later gave some £10,000 towards the running of the centre. In the next few weeks, the centre, now called Princess Mary House, was furnished and equipped by gifts from Guide companies all over Britain and from overseas. Today each room retains the name of the place which originally sponsored it, so you move past Dorset and through Buckinghamshire to reach India and Pakistan, while upstairs, Paisley is next door to Massachusetts.

Architecturally the house is one of the most curious we had ever seen. Look closely at the Georgian front and you will notice the top-storey windows are unglazed, merely painted in. Entering the front door, we found ourselves in a low-ceilinged, stone-flagged hall, part of the old Tudor cottage, but then entered Scotland, a beautiful white and gold drawing-room designed by Robert Adam. The house is full of these contrasts.

Up under the roof are two more Tudor rooms; one used as a chapel is full of dark beams and little corners, its dormer window looking out onto the back of the façade – a house of great character and much beloved by all who take training courses there, or camp on its sixty-five acres of parkland.

Guiders come from all over the world to train in this corner of the forest. If you think they spend their time learning campfire songs and tent pitching, Foxlease would soon put you right. The variety of skills includes of course those for which the forest background is ideal, such as archery, long-distance walking and riding, but there's also music and drama, craftwork and swimming, rifle shooting – the current Girl Guide report features parascending on its cover.

South of Foxlease we walked through Whitley Wood, where Brusher Mills once had his primitive shelter.

Once away from the car-park we met few people, no one in fact after a quarter of a mile, so perhaps the Lyndhurst area has improved in at least one respect since W.H. Hudson's time, for he wrote, 'Lyndhurst – the spot on which London vomits out its annual crowd of collectors, who swarm through all the adjacent woods and heaths with their vasculums, beer and treacle pots, butterfly nets, killing bottles and all the detestable paraphernalia of what they would probably call, "Nature study".'

Great oaks and beeches in heavy summer leaf cast a cool shade except where a giant had fallen. One huge beech had split off at its base, the wood so rotten you could crumble it with your fingers. In falling it had split open, to reveal the little round ball of a wren's nest all woven of moss and feathers. The stump of another beech was almost lost beneath the brown-streaked fans of a bracket fungus, and the grey bark of the hollies was scribbled with brown patterns left by the teeth of gnawing deer.

But across the fence, in New Park Inclosure, a new generation of trees was growing up. In 1949 the Forestry Commission were empowered to inclose twenty-acre regeneration plots, and here was one, about twenty-five years old. With deer, cattle and ponies prevented from grazing, young oak and beech had sprung up close together beneath a few older ones left as nurse trees: later they will be thinned to become forest giants in their time, say two hundred years hence.

Another wood we explored close to Lyndhurst was Brick Kilns. Here we came upon some forestry workers chopping very stubborn wood into logs – it proved to be the false acacias cut down at New Park and surely descended from Cobbett's beloved locust trees, very close textured and with a peculiar bitter smell. Better than this, we found some false acacia growing, drooping its graceful grey-green leaflets over a forest stream. No sign of any brickworks remained, but near the road some large, overgrown pits showed where the clay had been dug.

A little way along the road we went to see a modern kiln. Angels Farm Pottery has been open for ten years now. Visitors can come in and watch the potter at work or stroll round the shelves of finished pottery, doorknobs, tiny candlesticks, teapots, tall jugs all in soft country shades of browns, greys and moss green. Another range of jugs and plates in a different style, highly glazed, was decorated with forest motifs, ponies, deer and oak leaves, all lovingly crafted – it takes a day and a half to pack the kiln, twelve hours to fire it, with two days wait for it to cool down again. Most of the sales are here, direct to the public, which helps keep the price down, though some pieces are sent to Yaldhurst, the forest craft centre we had visited at Pennington.

Now it was time to say goodbye to Lyndhurst itself and explore the wide stretch of country eastwards. We went south to Ladycross, another of the old forest lodges, to walk through Frame Heath Inclosure, a very special area.

Mixed woodland of no great age slopes down to the north, cut into blocks by straight Forestry Commission gravel tracks and wide grassy rides, not particularly beautiful as a New Forest scene, but we had come in the evening, as we always do, and there as usual were the sika deer, a mother and calf just stealing out from the trees' shelter to graze in the open in the last rays of the sun. Soon two more hinds joined her, with their calves, each a lovely golden brown with lines of spots along the flanks though easy to miss among the bracken. In the next clearing a small herd of stags were grazing, constantly swishing their tails to ward off the evening flies.

Fallow deer can be seen anywhere in the forest, roe are shyest of all and red are scarce, but the sika stay on the whole faithful to this stretch of woodland and seldom seem to cross the Southampton to Bournemouth railway line, staying south of it in these mixed woods of pine and birch, oak and beech. There is often a lower storey of willow, hawthorn or holly scrub which gives them extra protection.

The first sika were brought to England from Japan in 1860: later some were released on various private estates including Beaulieu. Two stags and two hinds were freed into the forest from there in 1904, and from these two pairs are descended the herds we are watching today.

The stags in front of us broke off their grazing now and then to retreat to the wood's edge and thrash their antlers against the nearest branches, making a loud clattering. This is to scrape the velvet off – some had long strands of this soft outer skin hanging from their antlers, giving them a dishevelled look. However, soon it will be cleaned off and, coats in their foxy red prime, they will leave the herd and give all their attention to rutting, which, in the case of sika, takes place in September and October. When all the grunting and whistling and chasing is over and the deer are mated, stags, hinds and yearlings form mixed herds, staying together for the winter. Come the spring the stags leave to form their own herds while they shed their antlers and begin to grow new ones. The hinds calve in May and June, leaving their young alone, hidden in the undergrowth for quite long periods while they wander off to graze. The calves stay with their mothers for a year, until the next young are born.

A little owl screams close by, the deer graze on, undisturbed as twilight falls over Frame Wood, Moon Hill and Hawkhill, the sikas' little world.

If the woods are shabby in August, the great heathlands come into their own. East of Lyndhurst lie vast heathlands such as Matley, Yew Tree and northern Beaulieu. On a sunny morning they stretch away purple with heather to fringing trees or blue summer sky. To walk over the heaths is to discover they hold far more than just heather.

It would be foolish in fact to try to try to walk over some parts. Earlier in the year cottongrass sends up warning flags of silky white fluff where heath ends and bog begins. Round the upper reaches of Beaulieu River spreads Matley Bog, full of treasure to the botanist, though even in tall boots we sometimes had to pull each other out of the quaking mud so prettily and treacherously covered with sphagnum moss. Between its tufts grow round-leaved sundew, sending up small white flowers, its leaves edged with crimson hairs to entrap flies which it digests to make up for the lack of nitrogen in the soil. The showy gold stars of bog asphodel are past their prime, but the glowing orange seedheads are just as handsome. Bog pimpernel lays little shining trails of silvery green leaves across the moss.

The mud bubbled and stank but we squelched on, searching for the rare bog orchid, a tiny yellow flower. There were yellow buds of marsh St John's wort, yellow-flowered sedge and, on less swampy stretches, yellow tormentil ... To confuse one further, heath-spotted orchid had flowered there and seeded, leaving clumps of unmistakably orchid leaves spotted with purple. High overhead a lark sang and three black-headed gulls flew off down river to Beaulieu in a flash of white wings.

At last, in the very wettest part of the bog, almost in running water, we found the orchid, tall as a little finger, with tiny flower spike the colour of lady's bedstraw and inch-long leaves. It is a strange thing with elusive flowers: though you may know perfectly well what they look like, once the eye has rediscovered one, many more appear. There were quite a few orchids scattered through the bog, though never more than three growing close together.

Along the river there straggled a strange wood, England's nearest approach to the Everglades in Florida! The alders have been coppiced – that is, had their main stems cut out, so each has divided into four or five thin shoots, while their roots spread out dividing the stream into several different interweaving channels betweel black mud banks and islands of bright green grass, though in winter storms the whole stretch may be under water. These floods nourish the strips of heath on either side. Marsh ragwort was growing there and white valerian. In winter flocks of siskin descend on this alder carr to feed on the seeds.

As we walked up towards Matley Wood, the going became

firmer, bog myrtle and heather appeared, the cross-leaved heath all a-flicker with butterfly wings, a colony of silver-studded blue. On the wood's edge grew alder buckthorn, its berries beginning to turn orange, its leaves food for the caterpillars of brimstone butterflies. Matley's fine old oaks and birches shelter a small caravan site near the road.

Crossing the road brought us into Denny Wood and a much larger caravan site, but Denny is a huge wood, and once that is left behind we are among well-spaced ancient beeches, a few hollies, stretches of grass and bracken, pleasant walking country with sun and shade. The track leads us to Denny Lodge, a little enclave of cottages and a few pasture fields round a forest lodge, though this one replaced the original half-timbered house.

From here we set out to find the portraits at Woodfidley. Our way took us across open country, with grass and bracken, clumps of birches and flat, firm walking, a pleasure after the bog. Rounding a stand of bracken man high, we glimpsed in the distance five red deer hinds grazing with their calves. The tall beeches of Woodfidley commanded the view on our right. At one point we made a detour to search for another flower seldom seen.

Gladiolus illyricus belongs to the iris family and is very rare now, thought to grow only in the New Forest, where it likes to be right in under sheltering bracken. The day had turned really warm; the flies were out; the bracken stood from waist to shoulder high and there were acres of it, but at last, peering down under the tall fronds, we found a perfect scaled-down gladiola a foot high with iris-like leaves and two reddish purple flowers open on its spike. But two of us in two hours found only half a dozen whereas in former years there had been many more. If you do find this beautiful forest flower, please leave it to grow and if possible increase. We hoped it was some seasonal factor which had brought about its scarcity this year, rather than grasping hands.

The tall Woodfidley beeches on their hill are for some reason connected with rain; 'Woodfidley rain will last all day,' the saying goes, which presumably means rain from that direction, though it is difficult to work out the logic in this since

Woodfidley is north-west of Beaulieu but south-east of Lyndhurst!

We had come to photograph the carvings on the beech boles. They take some finding since the wood has a flourishing under storey of holly, growing often right up against the beeches. The story goes that the Irish labourers brought in to build the nearby railway had an unpopular overseer, so to get their own back they went into the woods and carved caricatures of him on the trees – and they are still there quite plain. The best shows a fat man in a top hat with a nose like Mr Punch; it must have been carved about 1852, on a beech already three hundred years old.

Coming down from the majestic trees of Woodfidley, we came out onto the heathland, miles of purple heather stretching away on every hand, breezy under a vast blue sky, an exhilarating place to walk. Ling, the common purple heather, covers much of the heath – it is all a-hum with bees: the reddish-purple flowers of bellheather grow on drier stretches, with here and there the pink cross-leaved heather going to seed, since it is the first to bloom. The large emerald-green caterpillars of the emperor moth graze on heather; it also provides nesting cover for larks, pippits and snipe. You can tell how recently the land has been burned by the height of ling – left alone it will grow into woody bushes three feet high.

Out on the heath we came upon a low bank stretching right across our path though broken away in parts and not easy to see at any distance since it too was overgrown with heather; moreover, it does not proceed in a straight line and the ditch that ran beside it has largely fallen in. This is Bishop's Dyke, which once enclosed some five hundred acres of heath and bog.

In 1284 John de Pontoise, Bishop of Winchester, petitioned Edward I for a grant of land from the New Forest and received the surprising answer that he could have as much as he could crawl round in a day. One variation on this folk tale suggest there were two bishops in competition: Joan Begbie in her delightful book *Walking the New Forest* gives her opinion as to how this bishop covered so much rough ground:

'The bishop devised himself a machine which would help him to cover a considerable area and still keep within the terms of the agreement. The machine consisted of two wheels with a sort of padded axle across which the bishop lay and propelled himself along at quite a respectable pace with his hands and feet. It is delicious to think of him bumping through the heather, struggling up the rises, free wheeling down the slopes and possibly coming a purler over a family of wild boar wallowing in the mud.'

Whatever his method, the land was given to Winchester diocese, so much is fact, but why should the bishop want a stretch of inaccessible heath? Some suggest it was once a lake coveted for its fish, others that its low-lying boggy nature made it good snipe-breeding country. Certainly it would not grow crops. Did the bishop want simply to run some ponies? Building bank and ditch by hand would have been a mighty work since both must have been much larger seven hundred years ago.

Little harebells grew here and there and yellow tormentil. Over on our left the slender trunks of birches that fringe Denny Wood shone silver pale in the sun. Somewhere out here we visited our secret colony of marsh gentian, beautiful sky-blue flowers lifted to the sky, another rarity, though we found to our great pleasure that last year's little group has increased to some twenty plants.

For the newcomer to the forest, overawed perhaps by its great woodlands and spreading heath, a few landmarks can provide reassurance. Woodfidley beeches on their knoll make a reference point, and the isolated clump of tattered pines at Shatterford, for which we were making. There is a picnic site under the trees; across the road lies Beaulieu Road station and close beside it the maze of wooden-railed pens which are the chief venue for pony sales. These begin in April and continue through till November.

Horse-boxes begin to arrive, drawing up in a wide arc on the grass, and soon ponies are being shoved or cajoled into the range of pens with labels stuck on their rumps. Around the edge, stalls are going up, and soon the smell of hot dogs mingles with pungent odours of dung, straw and horse. Other stalls sell saddlery, anoraks, boots and horse brasses, hot drinks and pork pies.

There are toddlers wandering round being shown 'nice horsy', elderly gypsies sizing up the stock with experienced eyes, pony club girls yearning for ponies, stewards in white coats sorting out the next entrants, and an RSPCA inspector keeping a watchful eye. Side deals are going on here and there, two or three gathered round a solitary pony, while a splendid stallion, dwarfing his lesser brethren, is led round to show off his points and book future appointments. Above the shouts and neighs and whinnies a train roars by up on the embankment, so that for one moment passengers glimpse the whole panorama of tossing manes and pens, tweed jackets and flat caps.

But all this is peripheral. The heart of the sale is of course the ring, a small railed enclosure with tiers of railway-sleeper steps round it and a raised desk with a roof for the auctioneer. When a pony is brought in, it is teased with a rag on a stick to make it buck and trot, so demonstrating its capabilities.

Bidding is brisk. Many ponies are bought up by the 'meat boys', as they're known in the forest, to be slaughtered for pet food. The lucky ones go to private homes to be broken in for riding, and eventually to trot once more the ferny forest tracks.

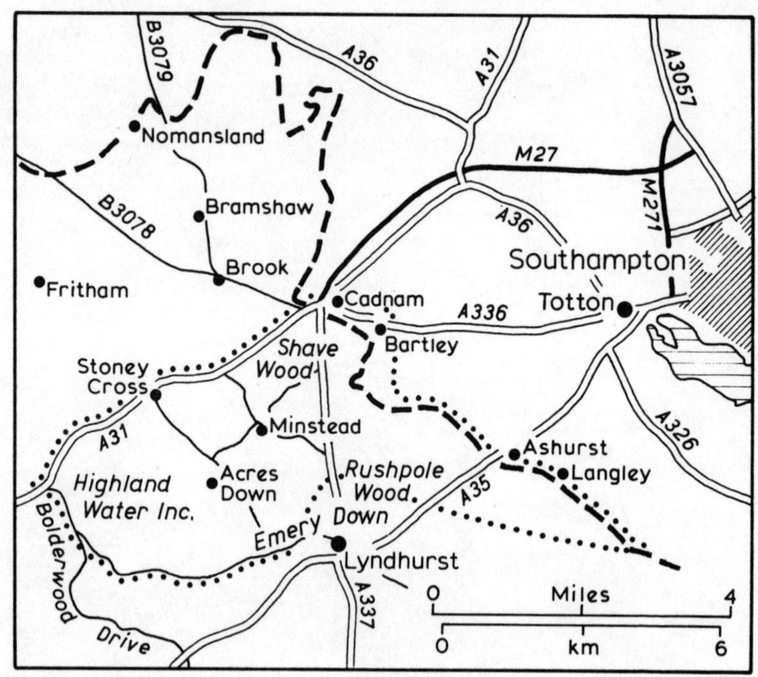

Around Minstead

7 *Around Minstead*

Thatched cottages in bright gardens along narrow, wandering lanes, an old church on the hill, a winding stream and one general store – of all the forest communities Minstead is the one nearest to the accepted picture of a pretty English village. Sheltered from the north by the hanging woods round Malwood, its green hollows and tall hedges, old trees and sudden bends hide away several mansions and the Manor House. Minstead makes a delightful centre from which to explore this north-east corner of the forest.

The oldest part of Minstead must be Castle Malwood to the north. Here, just below the thundering traffic of the A31, lie the wooded terraces of an Iron Age hill fort, a plateau of about four acres surrounded by ramparts of banks and ditches now partly eroded and carpeted with fallen leaves of many autumns but still quite easy to trace along its north-east side, which runs beside a lane. It is a surprise to find a house built in the middle of the fort, yet it was after all built to live in, a place of refuge for people with their domestic animals and stores when neighbouring tribes threatening attack.

For hundreds of years the fort has been the site of a forest lodge. Tradition tells that King Rufus slept here the night before his fatal hunting expedition, dreaming that blood poured from him and rose into the sky obscuring the sun itself. This seems to accord with the name Malwood, reeking of evil ... In fact the latest research, as we shall see in the next chapter, casts doubt on the entire theory that he *was* killed in Canterton, and Malwood is prosaically named after Godric Malf and his sons, who held Minstead at the time of the Domesday survey!

The present Malwood Lodge was built by Sir William Harcourt, at one time Home Secretary; in 1890, a rambling house of brick, half timbering and balconies. Today it stands divided into flats but half empty and neglected, amid overgrown lawns. Doubtless in the days of former owners such as the Duchess of Westminster this was a peaceful forest retreat: now the traffic noise is all invasive.

Just across the lane lies another Malwood Castle, only to be glimpsed through the rhododendrons, a vast house with high, ornate gables. This was built in 1802 though it has been much altered and enlarged since. In 1910 it was bought by Daniel Hanbury, of Allen & Hanbury, the baby-food makers, who threaded these narrow lanes in the first Rolls Royce 'Silver Ghost' to be seen in the forest. Today, surrounded by new buildings, it is owned by the Southern Electricity Board, who guard it with an invisible ray system, across the drive.

Walking down toward the centre of Minstead out of the woods, past a very small green and a turning to London Minstead, we came to the village hall, two large wooden buildings making an L shape. These were originally Army huts, given to Minstead by Daniel Hanbury in 1920. The grateful villagers presented an illuminated address of thanks signed by almost the entire population – so it was a deep shock to learn on the death of Mr Hanbury that the whole transaction had been made by word of mouth: no papers existed to validate the gift, and the hall must therefore be sold! It was bought by the District Council and Lady Congleton of Minstead Lodge for £6,000 on condition that the villagers eventually raised the money to buy it back – which they did, though it took some eleven years of fund-raising. At last in 1963 the loan was cleared and the huts were named Minstead Hall.

Now it is the centre of village life, housing among other societies the archery club, indoor bowls, Junior Minstead and the annual Flower Show which draws gardeners from all over the forest. Every summer there is a carnival and every winter a pantomime, its story chosen by the village children – the year we went it was called *Frankenstein*! The village fair includes traditional attractions such as craft stalls and a parade of Shire horses but comes right up to date with troops of majorettes and a parachute drop. Entering the shop, we saw a poster advertising the next barn dance – altogether Minstead glows with community spirit, even though some of the houses are now owned by newcomers who commute daily to Southampton.

Not so long ago, on the Isle of Wight, the proprietor of a village shop actually burst into tears because she could not supply a pair of red slippers, size five, so proud was she of their range of goods. The shop at Minstead does not actually sell slippers, but it certainly carries that tradition into the 1980s. Besides the usual range of groceries, it offered, in October, seeds, bulbs and pot plants with a bright line in cyclamen, pineapples and melons, apricot chutney and cranberry sauce, *lasagne verde* and poppadums, quails' eggs and Seyval Blanc Minstead, with locally baked crusty bread, a range of newspapers, *The Field* and *Homes and Gardens*; it is also the post office.

Shop, pub and a crossroads of lanes, one leading up to the church, form the small centre of the village: once the blacksmith's shop was here too, and the rectory. The pub has a very strange inn sign showing a creature with stag's feet, a human body, a donkey's head and a pig's snout. The original of the Trusty Servant hangs in Winchester College. Years ago an itinerant artist made a copy of it and took it into the Minstead pub, where the publican took a fancy to it and the artist got free beer – so the inn takes its name from its sign, 'going down the Trusty' being a familiar phrase. No one can seem to remember what it was originally called.

Much of Minstead once belonged to the manor: it is still a large estate south of the village. Conan Doyle, in *The White Company*, paints a picture of the house as it might have been in the fourteenth century, home of the Socman (or Squire) of Minstead: '... a broad green lawn where five cows lay in the sunshine and droves of black swine wandered unchecked. A brown forest stream swirled down the centre of this clearing with a rude bridge flung across it ... a second field sloped up to a long, low lying wooden house with thatched roof and open squares for windows. A wreath of blue smoke floated up through a hole in the thatch and a great black hound lay chained to the doorpost.'

A real manor house was built in 1719 by one Henry Compton, a wealthy jockey: in old prints it looks large and rather forbidding, but William Cavill, in his delightful little book *Portrait of a Forest Village*, remembered the manor with affection as it was early this century. 'The manor was a community in itself. It had a large staff to do all that was needed to keep everything in good order. Nobody overworked themselves, nobody had the sack and nobody was ever turned out. It always seemed to me like a big, benevolent institution.'

The Compton family provided rectors for Minstead, Canon John, the Rev. Charles and the Rev. John spanning the years 1842-1932. During the last war, the Royal Army Service Corps were billeted in the manor house, and afterwards it was found to be in such ruinous condition, it was pulled down, but, as at Brockenhurst, a new house has risen in its place.

A long, winding drive from the lodge leads between clipped-back walls of rhododendrons: on our last visit we had to pause for three cock pheasants to fly up and over them in their usual clumsy-looking way but adding their own green, red and gold to the autumn yellow of sweet chestnut and sycamore. Built in Beaulieu white brick (which is in fact a deep cream) and a copy of the old house, Minstead Manor looks from a little distance a real Georgian country seat, though it is a mere twelve years old. Built a little forward of the old site to avoid its cavernous cellars, the house looks out over gently sloping parkland, acres of grass with here and there a huge oak or cedar standing alone, to a far rim of woodland, a peaceful English scene little changed over the centuries.

Another stretch of drive brought us back into the village proper, the churchyard where the author of *The White Company* is buried, and the question, why is Arthur Conan Doyle's tombstone there when his last years were spent living in Sussex?

He was born in Edinburgh in 1859, trained as a doctor and worked on a whaler and in the slums of Birmingham before setting up his first practice in Southsea. Now he began to write short stories; his first novel, *A Study in Scarlet*, when Sherlock Holmes burst upon the world, was turned down three times but finally appeared in 1887. This was followed by *The White Company* and success in a new magazine called *The Strand*. One career pulled against the other until, lying in bed during an attack of flu, 'I determined with a wild rush of joy to cut the painter and to trust forever to my power of writing.'

Later in life he became an ardent spiritualist, travelling all over the world lecturing and writing, with his second wife, Jean. They eventually settled in Sussex but bought a cottage retreat deep in the New Forest. Today Bignell Wood is not so far from the A31 but still tucked away down a wooded drive and charmingly moated by the Cadnam River – you have to cross on a wooden footbridge. When the Doyles bought Bignell Wood, it was a mere one-storey cottage but they enlarged it, adding rooms upstairs – part of the new roof was flat. By this time Conan Doyle had gained a reputation for strangeness with the locals, through garbled accounts of his involvement in spiritualism. The children of his second marriage made the most of this, dancing on the roof at night and waving lights in a ghostly manner!

When Sir Arthur died, he was buried in the garden of their Sussex home, but the family moved to Bignell Wood, making it their permanent home until the early 1950s, and so they felt it more fitting to move the grave to the nearby churchyard of Minstead.

The cross stands under an old oak, on the brink of the hill, inscribed 'Steel true: blade straight', looking out over the manor woods which Conan Doyle evoked so well.

Minstead church is well known simply because it is such an unlikely building – with its dormer windows haphazardly set among the roof tiles, it resembles a cottage leaning against a tower – so it is no surprise to find the inside rich in curiosities. At the west end there survives not just a gallery but two of them, the higher probably to house the charity school children. Beside the famous three-decker pulpit stands a font so old its carvings are rough and inscrutable in message. What *is* this strange creature with the head of a lion and two bodies?

In 1893 Henry Abbot was doing some gardening at the Parsonage (now the Old Rectory) when his fork seemed to strike a rock. Digging further, he unearthed the font and after cleaning it up wheeled it up to the church on his wheelbarrow. Carved in Norman or even Saxon times, it must be one of the oldest fonts in England. It was probably buried for safety during the Reformation, or possibly hidden from Cromwell's Puritans.

The homely atmosphere created by the dormer windows continues inside, where different areas 'belonged' to different families. The south aisle was added in 1790 for the Compton family and their tenants at the manor: Minstead Lodge had a private family pew on the north side: entered from the porch, this was like a separate chapel and now houses the organ, but the Castle Malwood pew remains just as it was, a small, square room with comfortable seats, a black-leaded fireplace and, on our last visit, the final domestic touch, a jug of dahlias on the mantelpiece.

From the church on its hill a footpath leads down into the valley through a copse overlooking the spread of manor wood to a ford across the stream known here as Fleetwater. Beside it stands the village school building. This was the nearest school to Shave Green, where there was a large gypsy camp: few of the children had macs and would arrived soaked from the long walk on rainy days, so their outer clothing was stripped off and hung all day in the rafters to dry out – some natives of Minstead can still remember the 'laundry smell'!

When the school was closed, the building was converted into a Rural Studies Centre, the first in Hampshire. School parties can come and stay to sample life in the country: the great woods and heaths around must open up new worlds to children from Portsmouth or Southampton. Another rambling lane past its gate leads us to every visitor's goal in Minstead, Furzey Gardens.

For hundreds of years this was a rough hillside bearing gorse, bramble and one small thatched cottage, built in 1560. This remains, has been un-modernized and stands today much as it did at the turn of this century with a huge brick fireplace and low ceilings of rough, dark beams. These timbers came from the

Tudor shipbuilding yard at Lymington, the floorboards upstairs being the size cut for deck boards. It is all very handsome now, wood gleaming from polish, horse brasses and pottery ornamenting walls and windowsills, but it must have been very different at the turn of the century, when a family with fourteen children lived here. They used a ladder then to reach the upper floor and had to fetch their water from the hillside. G.I. Macfarquhar's interesting guide to Minstead says, 'They no doubt slept on straw on the floor. It was customary for such large families to sleep in a row with the youngest boy or girl in the middle and graded out to the eldest at each end.'

Furzey House itself is altogether grander, though carrying on the same tradition, a long, low house with many eye-browed windows set in its deep thatch and tall brick chimneys. Built in 1922 for the Dalrymple brothers, this is said to be the largest thatched roof in Hampshire: from its hillside the house looks out over the gardens and right across the New Forest to the far downs of the Isle of Wight. To make the gardens on the infertile forest clay, cart loads of soil were brought in and paths cunningly laid out to weave informally up, down and round to little glens and dells among the trees or to a summerhouse or lake, making the gardens seem much larger than their eight acres.

After the death of the last Dalrymple, the house was let and the gardens became neglected, until bought by the Selwood family in 1972, since when they have been restored and opened to the public. In spring there are drifts of crocus, narcissus and miniature daffodil under the trees; in summer rhododendrons and azaleas make a blaze of colour. In October, even so late in the year, the gardens were bright with dahlias, tall white-flowered *Euchryphia* and everywhere the heathers for which it is famous: there is even one bred here, *Erica Furzey*.

Down in one corner beneath the trees stood a small village of child-sized houses, all built of wood with four-foot doors and stairs inside. The lake, crossed by rustic bridges, is stocked with golden orfe, rudd and carp: the fernery is intended to grow every native British fern – there is a pleasant variety to explore, otherwise one can just sit on one of the many benches and enjoy the peaceful, fragrant scene.

Before leaving Furzey we went to see the Will Selwood Art and Craft Gallery, housed in a specially built thatch and timber building like a barn, set up in 1974 to display the work of local artists and craftsmen. (Commission on sales and all the profits from Furzey go to charity.) Here there were watercolours of forest scenes, pottery, scraper-board pictures of deer and pony; most striking of all, and some pieces so large they could only be accommodated in the yard outside, were chairs and tables each hollowed out of one block of wood with no joints at all and beautifully finished to show off the natural grain and colour.

'The beauty of these gardens is a reflexion of God's love and man's creative co-operation with God,' says a notice by the gate.

Leaving Furzey we moved east right across the village, to the part called London Minstead, to call on Minstead Lodge, which in spite of the distance is closely linked with Furzey.

A winding wooded drive leads up to what appears at first to be a rather forbidding great house, built in the eighteenth century, but this is really the back. The front, tall, gabled and with splendid two-storey bay windows, looks out onto a formal terrace and beyond to fields and a wide view into the forest, a house of fitting dignity for that private pew. It was home at one time to the Duncan family, Dr Duncan being physician to Queen Victoria. In this century it went through a period of neglect before being bought by a charitable trust set up by Mr Tim Selwood, owner of Furzey Gardens, in memory of his brother Peter who was killed in a flying accident. The propeller from his aeroplane is set up on the lawn as a striking memorial.

The Lodge is now run as a community with broadly Christian outlook though undenominational. Its aims are to improve the quality of life, safeguard our environment and resources, promote aid to famine areas abroad and to the handicapped in this country, and foster understanding between differing religions. In practice this means about fifteen people resident at the Lodge, each one responsible for some part of the work of running house and estate – seventeen acres of gardens, the forge, goat pens, woodwork shops, henhouses, an immense greenhouse, a vast walled vegetable plot and of course cooking for the community. This is often augmented by parties of visitors. On our last visit they were expecting a party of disabled from a poor district of London. The previous week visitors from Poland had rebuilt a rockery and flight of stone steps, for everyone is expected to use their particular skills.

What a fascinating experiment in living to find tucked away on the forest edge of Minstead, yet accessible to all. For anyone may apply to come and stay for a few days at the Lodge. You are expected to join in the work programme until lunchtime; after that you are free for the rest of the day, with an evening meal if required – no money changes hands. At this time of year there is a great deal to be done to preserve the garden harvest, beans to be salted, vegetables and fruit to be prepared for the freezer, herbs to be dried. A friend of ours who had recently stayed for three days spent every morning making plum jam, but this is a small price to pay for the chance of exploring a new way of life, and the Lodge is not just a period house in a peaceful setting: there is a library, swimming-pool, squash court, children's playground, even a chapel, informally furnished with straw bales for seats.

Just outside the gate stands a small white building, 'The Studio', belonging to Little London Spinners. Here you can buy hand-spun clothes, wool or spinning equipment, watch demonstrations or even take spinning lessons.

West of Minstead along the road to Emery Down lies a district called Skymers: this appears on old maps as Scheimers, which one forest writer suggests means they were tricky customers in these parts encroaching land from the forest! Traditionally, if you could raise a cottage between dusk and dawn, with smoke coming out of the chimney as the sun rose, you could keep it – and a garden as well if you had managed to fence it round. But one would hesitate to mention squatters now in this neighbourhood: on one side of the road heathland spreads away toward high woods: on the other pine trees and rhododendrons hide prosperous modern houses set in their own grounds.

Little Skymers is one of these, the home of the Minstead wine, Seyval Blanc. The vineyard was planted on a gentle easterly slope in 1980. Black polythene over the ground keeps weeds down and warmth in; black thread twined invisibly among the vines keeps off most of the marauding birds. This month the grapes had just been harvested and sent off to be pressed. They have to be picked after a dry night, as dew would dilute the sugar content. Sun shone down on the rows of vines; pochard and Carolina ducks called from the pond nearby – the owner could relax now until pruning begins in January. The tradition of wine-making in the forest goes right back to the monks of Beaulieu, of course: there is another small vineyard on the western edge at North Gorley.

Returning to the pond, we crossed over to Andrew's Mare car-park to visit another pond. We wandered along rabbit paths in the heather down a wide slope of heath with views across to Bolderwood and Highland Water Inclosure, to an elbow of stream in Withybed Bottom, where bog asphodel raised its orange seedpods and toadstools the size of saucers, sinister and pale, grew in the shade of holly clumps. Bushes of heather elbow high showed this slope had not been burned off for a long time: here and there little devil's bit scabious and sprigs of bellheather still held a brave hint of colour. As we circled round and began to climb back up the ridge, bracken took over the drier soil, tawny, yellow and gold, a last fling before frost brings winter brown to the heath.

On the top of the ridge lies the pond with wildly indented edge, all little peninsulas and bays: in fact it is another flooded gravel working and a site reserved, like Setley, for model powerboat racing, though here the heathland surroundings and wide views make a more attractive setting.

Car-drivers, streaming along the A31 just above us, notice Stoney Cross only as a garage and a pub – the Compton Arms named after the family which for so long provided the squires of Minstead. Once Stoney Cross Airfield and Canterton would have been considered part of the village – now they are effectively cut off from it by the dual carriageway. The only way north is to go east through the lanes to the vast roundabout at Cadnam.

So we turn south and off along a narrow lane, crowded only with quiet brown cattle browsing on the banks, to Acres Down, a grassy hillside scattered with huge old oaks and beeches, here and there a clump of holly bright with berries or a birch, leaves turning brilliant yellow. The track dips down, curving round a half moon of grass. Under an oak stands a little clump of false death cap, a pale yellow toadstool patched with white: it is said not to be poisonous (the real death cap is fatal) but the strong earthy smell is hardly inviting. Close by, a fallen beech is being slowly, very slowly, digested by the earth. Rain rots it away, mice and voles tunnel through the softened bark, moss invades the crevices, and fern roots in the moss, while fungus spreads all through its fibres – here the sulphur tuft is beginning to send up its fruiting bodies to the surface, tiny strings of amber beads which will grow into finger-high fungi, deep orange in the centre, a lovely autumn decoration among the green mosses.

A loud rustling in the undergrowth, too clumsy-sounding for deer, but we look up hopefully and there is an enormous barrel-shaped sow and a whole litter of tiny piglets cavorting round her, knocking each other over and squeaking with excitement at this new freedom. They are Wessex Saddlebacks with black shoulders and rumps, pink in the middle. Mum proceeds more slowly, intent on rootling up acorns and beech mast.

Long ago wild boar would have been a common sight in the forest, though they must have died out by the seventeenth century, for Charles I decided to reintroduce them, bringing stock from Germany. John Aubrey said, 'They much increased and became terrible to the travellers.' Also they fraternized with the natives. 'They tainted all the breed of pigges of the neighbouring partes, which are of their colour; a kind of soot colour.' These seem to have perished during the lean times of the Civil War.

In the great forests of France, boar still roam wild. Covered in coarse brown hair even to the tip of the tail, with a paler face, the sows roam in herds with their striped young ones, while the boars remain solitary except for the breeding season. Though they are hunted and their bite is terrible, most of the time they rootle about the woodland floor peacefully enough, devouring roots, carrion and of course acorns in autumn.

Here the traditional pannage season begins in September, its length depending on the size of the acorn crop. This ancient right has a dual purpose, to fatten the pigs and to decrease the amount of acorns and mast lying on the forest floor, for too many acorns in the diet of ponies or cattle can lead to death. In this particular year there has been a record crop of every kind of wild fruit, so there is great concern over this problem and already pony deaths have been reported. Part of the trouble is that far fewer pigs are now let out on the forest. At Acres Down Farm they were so worried that their cattle had been brought in recently in a drift, or round-up, all two hundred of them, while thirty pigs were sent out to mop up acorns.

Shirley Holms, the rare breed centre, at one time bred Tamworths, a rather long-snouted pig with a sinister expression and some slight resemblance to the ancient native pig; these had to be withdrawn from the forest because of widespread complaints of wild boar being let loose!

The sow had eaten her fill, lay down in the sun in the lea of a fallen birch and dozed off. Bracket fungus stood out from the silver bark in rounded shelves, black in the middle, shading out to fawn edges, like velvet to touch. The age of the Acres Down trees makes this a splendid hunting ground for fungi and leads also to strange habits of growth. Years ago a great beech had fallen, dragging its roots high out of the ground: from the top of them springs a birch eight feet tall. Another beech had become so hollow it had split into two halves so that you could walk between them, and each continued to grow independently. A third tree groaned and muttered to itself – you could hear it from several yards away. Many trees creak or scrape branches of course, but this oak 'talked' only when the breeze was still.

Here close by under a group of birches was growing that most painted of all fungi, fly agaric, flaming scarlet with white patches, every pixie's favourite castle, though actually poisonous.

Where the land dipped down into a hollow we could see a patch of bright yellow between the tree boles – at a distance it looked like a bed of chrysanthemums. This was bog myrtle whose fragrant leaves turn these lovely autumn shades of lemon and tangerine.

A gate led into Highland Water Inclosure and a change of atmosphere, for this is largely conifer – we walk between soaring, regular lines of Corsican and Scots pine, young trees compared with Acres Down, casting deep shade over the brown forest floor.

Here the fungi are fewer, though coral spot grows on fallen twigs and close by a boletus with a sticky brown top, nicknamed Penny Bun fungus. All the boletus have tubes instead of gills; the underside of the Penny Bun resembles yellow foam rubber. On our way back we found saffron milk cap, a short, chubby fungus with a wavy edge, carrot-coloured but ringed with dark green. When bruised, the flesh itself turns dark green and exudes milk. The earliest known drawing of a fungus is that of saffron milk cap, decorating the wall of a villa in Herculaneum, a fresco dating from the first century AD.

Thump, skitter, squeal – the piglets were running a private Derby through the bracken, except for one who had discovered the delight of rasping his little backside on an oak stump.

We left Acres Down to discuss the acorn problem and others with one of the two Forestry Commission Head Keepers.

The earliest guardians of forest law were called Tinemen; after the Office of Woods was set up, they were known as Woodmen Keepers; now the title of Keeper, as here defined, is unique to the New Forest – elsewhere the office would be Head Ranger. Jack lives in a cottage surrounded by chrysanthemums and beyond that by the woods. He works no fixed hours, reckons to be out five days a week but is on call twenty-four hours a day, every day, and in high season often works far into the night. (In spite of this the office of keeper often stays in a family, descending from father to son, such is the spell of the forest.) His main job concerns the welfare of the deer, but it also includes controlling the public, seeing the byelaws are obeyed, catching poachers and restoring lost children to their parents.

During the winter each keeper and underkeeper finds out how many deer there are on his beat, also their species and condition. In spring a complete deer census is taken and from that a shooting plan worked out for the whole forest, detailing how many must be culled. Keepers take individual culls of males in

August and September, and of females from November to February. All the time they are looking for weedy specimens, poor antlers and signs of disease or injury. There are four deer larders where the carcases are gralloched and jointed: butchers tender for the venison.

The last survey showed fifty to sixty red deer. Fallow are by far the most common, but the beautiful, shy roe seem to be in some decline, numbering about four hundred. There is anxiety that the actual work of the Forestry Commission in felling and moving timber has upset the roe, since a family likes to stay together, undisturbed in a permanent territory of some twenty acres.

Keepers work closely with the police in trying to catch poaching gangs. These use vans and fast cross-bred lurchers or deerhounds: they can also listen in to the keepers' VHF radio link with the police. A deer carcase can be worth £1 per pound weight, but it is not enough for poachers to be seen chasing deer with dogs: they must be caught red-handed to be convicted, when the fine can be £500 plus another £200 for each carcase.

Since fox-hunting helps keep nature in balance in the forest, accounting for some forty brace a year, keepers work with the hunt, enforcing a 'stopping' code – that is, seeing that earths blocked or stopped for a hunt are cleared after, or clearable by a fox. This also means they have to cope with hunt saboteurs. Other problems they have to deal with are youths zooming round heath or woodland paths on motorbikes, upsetting the wildlife, litter, especially round the car-parks, boys with airguns popping off at anything that moves, and the ever-present danger of fire.

Though the camp wardens are largely responsible for their own sites, the keepers help check them and at bank holidays carry out night patrols covering every single car-park, chiefly to stamp out illicit fires, since a single spark could cause a major disaster. At the height of the holiday season there can be five thousand trailers and tents in the forest.

'A dog is a hunter, you can't get away from that,' Jack said thoughtfully, rubbing the ears of his black labrador. One keeper we had talked to was so incensed at the harm caused by dogs –

a pregnant doe chased till she dropped a dead fawn, for example – that he wanted all dogs banned. All the inclosures have notices on the gates stating 'dogs on leads'. 'But people look round a stretch of wood, think whatever harm can he do, and let the dog off very often. Quite understandable really,' Jack went on. 'They just don't realize there may be ground-nesting birds, or a new-born fawn quite defenceless hidden in the bracken.'

Outside the inclosures dogs can run free of course, providing they don't chase the commoners' ponies or cattle.

Keepers also control the small amount of shooting which is allowed. Some two dozen permits are issued a year, though only to reputable locals; even then they must shoot only from 10 a.m. to sunset, having first apprised the relevant keeper of where and when. They have to keep away from car-parks and ponds where duck nest. The victims can be rabbits and pigeons, squirrels, crows and magpies, woodcock and cock pheasant.

To detail a keeper's work make him sound like a mere forest policeman, but this is far from true. Jack, like most keepers, has a deep love for and knowledge of his territory, knows every fox earth and badger sett and where a roe family has settled for the winter. Much of his work is positive, looking after the wild creatures' welfare, especially deer, educating visitors and assisting with the various surveys which are always going on to increase our understanding.

Not everyone thinks of the New Forest as a vast outdoor laboratory, but at any one time there will be several university teams studying some aspects of wildlife: lately there have been projects on the rare Dartford warbler, hobbies and sparrowhawks, and the feeding habits of fallow deer.

'Keeping the balance, that's what it's all about,' Jack said, as we left for a walk in Rushpole Wood.

Here the balance once toppled into fierce controversy, though on a golden October evening only spiralling larks disturbed the air. We crossed a stretch of delightful country half heath, half wood, heather and bracken fringed with slender birch, trunks shining silver. On the right, old shrubby heather bushes grew two feet high, splendid cover for meadow pippits, harriers and partridges: on the other side, the heather had been burned the previous year and was fresh green, good grazing and the height preferred by woodlarks. Whortleberry grew here and there, its leaves turning red now. In the West Country the berries are still gathered for pies, but in the forest the bushes are so heavily grazed, they seldom grow large enough to fruit.

A half-sunken path leads into woodland, the land full of ridges and hollows, old beeches, oaks and hollies, with here and there an open glade where sunlight greens the forest floor round a fallen giant. Little sandy paths printed with horseshoe patterns wind in and out across small stretches of heath or open grassland or dark holly thickets. Ragwort fringes a carpet of fading bracken with bright yellow, and mountain ash droop branches heavy with berries that glow fiery orange in the sunset.

Here the Forestry Commission decided to thin the mature trees and stimulate good seed production: this caused a great outcry that a fine wood was being destroyed for financial gain, and the woodland floor further damaged by the dragging of heavy logs – one of the latest conflicts between the Forestry Commission and local residents.

One fallen beech sprouts the pearly brackets of oyster fungus; further on we find the shiny brown tops of cepe, a fungus much prized on the Continent for its nutty flavour. A late speckled wood butterfly flits off down a ride, tempting us to follow towards Buskett's Lawn or Ironshill, Woodlands or Goldenhayes. Earlier in the year this is a good place for watching that handsome visitor the redstart. Further on, small hillocks are covered with self-sown Scots pine, anything from two to eight feet tall. A flock of missel thrushes planes over and disappears into the heather – Rushpole is a real walker's wood with something new round every wind of the path.

Lucky to see one butterfly in October, but soon we were to see hundreds, travelling further east, through Ashurst on the eastern border to the groves and garden of the New Forest Butterfly Farm.

You appreciate Ashurst better approaching from the opposite direction, passing first through the urban wilderness of Totton, *then* the village appears as the first sign of country with, at least, green verges and a view of trees. The main road is lined with

House and Garden: Furzey House

Burley Manor Hotel in winter

Exbury House

Old House in spring

Inchmery House

newish houses, a straight line of shops, garages, while behind it lie vast estates of commuter housing, a dormitory for Southampton, only seven miles away.

In spite of its pretty woodland name, the place seems too new and towny to be part of the forest, yet the name, variously spelled, goes back hundreds of years. In 1314 for example, Robert de Raundes seized Walter Puke, for trying to make off with some wood, which was against the forest laws. 'A cart of whitethorn valued 6d which he had cut down at a place called Asshurst. Therefore the sherrif is ordered to make Walter attend to answer both for the value and the offence.'

Hidden away in Ashurst Woods is a large campsite with room for nearly three hundred caravans. This is a Class A – that is, with maximum facilities including special features for the disabled, but no dogs allowed. However, we take a side turning toward Longdown on the forest boundary.

When the price of oil made indoor tomato-growing uneconomic, a Guernsey grower turfed out his plants and filled the hothouse with butterflies. This idea spread to the Langley Estate, and the New Forest Butterfly Farm was opened in 1981, most fittingly by Wendy Craig, star of the television series *Butterflies* – 'an indoor tropical garden filled with exotic free-flying butterflies and moths from around the world', as the brochure says.

The huge glasshouse is so full of flowers and the sound of splashing water, luxuriant creepers and flickering bright wings that you can almost forget that this is indoors, and imagine yourself in the steamy air of a jungle glade. Butterflies striped black and white like zebras flit over banks of bright petunias and zinnias or perch confidently on your sleeve, black swallowtails with electric blue spots rest on pink balsams, others with red and white markings seek out a lemon tree, and orange heliconiums flicker round the passionflower vines on which they breed. There are species here from South America, Africa, Asia and Australia: one of the largest is the Atlas moth with its eight-inch wing span, and all intricately patterned like a tapestry.

Of course none of these are, strictly speaking, New Forest butterflies, but the native varieties are catered for also, in a

Brockenhurst Manor Gardens

temperate area of their own. These are confined to breeding cages but their progeny will be released outside to increase our dwindling native stock. Here in glass-fronted cages were Painted Lady, Adonis Blue and Camberwell Beauty, their food plants growing with them. In the summer the caterpillars of the now rare swallowtail were found feeding on carrot in a forest garden. The whole clump was carefully dug up and removed to a cage here; in ideal conditions, fifteen of them pupated.

All round, among the buddleias, lantanas and vines, are other creatures on display. A glass window in a tree trunk reveals the inner workings of a bee's nest: a tank full of ferns holds locusts, while for those seeking a chill down the spine there are bird-eating spiders from Colombia, scorpions and the Mexican red-kneed tarantula. The hatching cage draws a crowd all day. Some of the pupae are so large that they resemble bats hanging up, and it is fascinating to watch one begin to split and some gorgeous creature slowly emerge from the drab bundle.

Among the waterlilies in the pond are terrapin, little hand-sized water tortoise, and free among the flowers, though shy and not often seen, are several Chinese quail, kept especially to hunt the spiders whose webs can destroy butterflies all too easily.

Outside, where the air strikes cool, there is a chain of small ponds fringed with water mint and mimulus, willow herb and rushes laid out to encourage our native dragonflies – a strange, naked-looking creature, an axolotl, lurks in one of them. Elsewhere there are cafés and gift shops, a putting course, an adventure playground for children and a garden centre. Each year there is a new feature, the latest being rides into the woods in traditional-shaped wagons drawn by Shire horses. There are also five acres of mature woods with wooden benches and tables scattered about for picnics, and shade doubly welcome after a morning in the tropics, as it were. Everything here is on the flat, so completely accessible for both prams and wheelchairs – one could well spend a whole day among the butterflies.

Moving north along the forest boundary, we passed on our left the stretch of woods north of Rushpole and came to Bartley to see the end product of some forest timber.

Bartley is a scattered village on the forest boundary. The best way to find Bartley Pottery, since it does not advertise its presence, is to look among the treetops for the unmistakable shape of kiln chimneys.

Inside the gate we are shown the kilns themselves, hand-built of brick in 1979, heated by four fire boxes, the fuel for which lies all around, stacked ten feet high. Timber from the forest is sent to the sawmills at Nursling, near Southampton, where the bark is sliced off together with a narrow crescent of wood. These slices are then brought back to Bartley to fire the kilns, so nothing is wasted. The pottery is on a different scale to that at Angel Farm, large ornamental garden pots in terracotta, some imposingly tall to flank some spacious terrace – the one being worked on the wheel took ten pounds of clay. Though a few people see the range of pots over the gate, wander in and make the odd purchase, Bartley Pottery is not really open to the public. All the pots are sold wholesale, mostly to garden centres within a twenty-mile radius, though a few are sent to London.

Leaving the autumn tang of woodsmoke behind, we made for the real woods again, in search of squirrels. Though we had glimpsed a few in all our forest walking, keepers and commoners alike agreed it was a poor year as far as numbers were concerned. (The Forestry Commission would call this a *good* year, considering the damage squirrels wreak on their trees!) Other years there has been the swish of a tail round every tree: no one knows why the numbers fluctuate in this strange way. Will this autumn with its remarkably rich crop of nuts and acorns result in a population explosion next year? Or does some disease step in to control their number?

Tumps of bright green moss grow between the snaking roots of old beeches in Shave Wood, among them the red caps of a fungus belonging to the russula family. A robin sings on a holly bright with berries as if posing for a Christmas card; there are little violet toadstools called Amethyst Deceiver, and more russulas, also a deep violet colour, but as yet no squirrels.

One group of hollies has its bark hanging off in long, frayed strips, the work of fallow bucks threshing about with their antlers, for the rutting season is just beginning. Descending a slope we come to more open and very wet, almost marshy ground where tall, slender Tawny Grisette is growing under a stand of birch, and honey fungus eats away at a beech stump. Here at last in the fork of an oak was the round nest or drey of a grey squirrel, and we sat down on the fallen beech to wait for the tenant.

There are no red squirrels in the forest now: most years one or two are reported, but they invariably turn out to be grey ones in their prime of fur, when head and flanks can shine reddish in sunlight. The nearest red squirrels are on the Isle of Wight, where there are no grey, although the red with their distinctive ear tufts were the original indigenous population of the whole of Britain.

In 1876 a small group of grey squirrel was brought over from America as a curiosity and released in Cheshire, where they began to breed. At that time, since no one had had the chance to assess what damage they could do to trees, they were regarded as charming little creatures, and so more were brought over. A later introduction was at Bournemouth, where they throve amid the pines and eventually spread to the New Forest in the 1940s. From time to time the native reds were stricken with a disease which severely reduced their numbers. Because one of these periodic declines in numbers coincided with the arrival of the grey, it was held for a long time that the greys drove the reds away: this theory is no longer fashionable. There seems no real evidence that grey actually fought with red, yet it is strange that the red squirrel still flourishes on the Isle of Wight and Brownsea Island in Poole Harbour where it has no competition.

For a long time, watching from our fallen tree, we saw nothing – in fact we *heard* the first sign of squirrel life, a harsh scratching sound from a distant beech, claws on bark, and soon a branch dipped lightly overhead as a grey squirrel swung onto it, ran down, turned round so that his tail stood up against the trunk, sat on his haunches and proceeded to eat a nut, turning the shell round and round in his nimble fingers, chiselling it off to reach the kernel.

Presently the squirrel whipped off up the tree and was lost to view in the high branches and we prepared to move, not expecting to see him again, when he, or another, suddenly appeared round the roots of a nearby oak, bright-eyed and busy picking up acorns. For a moment he froze, head up, tail up, then reassured dropped his stores, scrabbled a shallow hole and buried an acorn, all achieved at great speed as if he had an urgent appointment. Later in the year, when all the surface nuts have been eaten up, he will find the buried ones by smell. Far from hibernating in winter, as used to be thought, the coldest months are the busiest for the grey squirrel, late December and January being their mating season. There is much whisking of tails and racing about in high treetops, sometimes with several males chasing one female, pausing now and then to threaten each other with a chattering sound while the female screams to egg them on.

Once pregnant, the female sets about refurbishing her drey. This is a ball of small twigs and leaves usually in the fork of an oak, though the most snug dreys of all – and the safest – are built inside hollow trees. Having lined it with dry grass, the expectant mother spends some time in it: the babies are born in 6½ weeks, tiny, naked, blind and deaf, so it is another ten weeks or so before they are sufficiently grown to venture outside the drey, timing their arrival nicely to late primroses or early bluebells, the woods in their spring glory and, what is really important, plenty of juicy leaf buds. A few squirrels breed again around midsummer, three babies being an average litter.

The shadow of a crow skimmed across the clearing, and our squirrel shot off up the nearest beech. They have no real enemies in the forest except man: keepers have to hold numbers within check or no young trees would reach maturity; as it is, many grow deformed and so useless for timber through having bark or the main shoot nibbled off.

At least squirrels are not hunted for food anymore. It used to be the custom to go squirrel-hunting on Boxing Day, bringing them down out of the treetops with a weighted stick called a squoyle. Cooked, they were said to taste like rabbit, though these would have been red squirrels. The greys are reputed to be even tastier.

Our grey friend did not return, so we made our way northwards to Cadnam, known to every passing motorist for its roundabouts, one small of many years standing, one huge and new, syphoning traffic away from the village, leaving it a quiet backwater.

For there is a village, away from the main road with its red brick and garish petrol stations. Along the lanes there are old tiled cottages behind hedges bright with rose hips and trails of red briony, Cadnam River in its leafy windings, several shops, one of which has a fine range of beechwood chairs outside and makes furniture to order, and two pubs, the White Hart and Sir John Barleycorn, one of the most attractive we had seen in the forest, long, low and thatched, with windowboxes *over* the windows spilling out begonias and geraniums in a shower of colour against the whitewashed walls.

Behind the village lies Cadnam Green, a long, narrow, grassy space where ponies and donkeys graze, with farms here and there – flat fields spreading away. You can tell we are on the very forest edge here. And for all the occasional thatch roof and wandering geese, the motorway is present all the time as a constant roar of traffic: even from the green you can glimpse lorries apparently speeding through the treetops, as here the road is elevated above the village.

Yearning for the 'real' forest, we retreat north to Cadnam Common, a stretch of open country patched with gorse bushes, clumps of bramble with leaves turning scarlet and isolated birches shedding yellow leaves. Little milk cap toadstools grow in the grass, shiny brown like toffee, and spongy yellow boletus. In a flicker of chestnut and white, a flock of long-tailed tits settled on a bramble bush, 'tissing' gently to each other, but suddenly alarmed by wild cries they flit away.

And no wonder, for the common is invaded by galloping horses, herds of ponies and shouting humans – time for the autumn drift or round-up. These take place all over the forest through September and October. Visitors to the forest often think of the ponies as wild, but of course every single one is owned by a commoner and its fee must be paid each year.

We had come to take photographs; otherwise this is really no spectator sport but a strictly working occasion, and an unwary newcomer could easily get hurt. If you want to watch a drift, keep off open ground and stand against thick bushes or trees – we found a birch, and just in time, for, with drumming of hooves worthy of a Western, whinnies and neighs, a bunch of ponies careers past, driven at full tilt by galloping riders on both flanks, shouting and yelling at tops of voices. Unless the ponies are kept running at speed, the bunch will break up and some escape.

This time about a dozen are safely driven into a bottleneck with bushes along one side and a human fence on the other. With some cursing, grunting and slapping of rumps they are eventually all driven into a wooden pen and the gate swung to. Now the commoners at last have a chance to look over stock: some mares have foals running with them not seen before. The ridden horses steam gently, begin to graze now the excitement is over.

In the pen the ponies jostle and whinny, unused to being confined, strawberry roan and chestnut, light bay and rich bay with a white star, blue roan and grey. There is one black colt which will eventually grow into a white pony like its mother. Now the real business of the day begins: each pony must be wormed, branded and tail cut to show its fee has been paid. As each district of the forest has its own distinctive cut, this also serves as an address. Someone climbs up onto the rails and perches there with a clipboard, boys wander about making small fires with twigs – it all looks deceptively casual.

The worming is comparatively easy. A commoner climbs into the pen, shoves his way through a heaving sea of pony, finds his own and squeezes a plastic syringe into the side of its mouth while it tries to jump away, rear or toss its head. An Agister begins to trim tails, then one by one each pony is branded with its owner's initials or official mark – the brands have been heating up in the wood fires.

Then it is time for each owner to decide the future of his stock. Most of the ponies look in good condition, with glossy coats and well-rounded rumps, as they should be after the summer, but one mare is lame, another thin and showing her pin bones: horseboxes are backed up so these can be taken back home. Others are candidates for Beaulieu Pony Sales, and they are also sent off in horseboxes, while the lucky ones are allowed back onto the forest for another year of freedom, running out with glad whinnies through the reek of scorched hair and horse dung.

Where did the New Forest pony come from? There is, of course, that delightful tale that its forbears were horses which swam ashore from the wrecked ships of the Spanish Armada, but the breed must be far older than 1588, perhaps reaching back to prehistoric times, when truly wild horses roamed Britain: from those small, hardy ancestors are descended the breeds known today as Dartmoor, Exmoor and New Forest, though the story is a tangled one.

There were 'wild horses' pastured in the forest before William proclaimed it his new hunting ground in the eleventh century; for hundreds of years commoners have exercised their rights to run ponies. Not until the last century was any attention given to improving the strain. In 1852 Queen Victoria lent the Verderers a grey Arab stallion called Zorah which was stabled at New Park. In the 1890s Lord Arthur Cecil introduced stallions into the forest from Highlands, Cumberland, Dartmoor, Exmoor and later from Wales, which would seem to produce a real mongrel pony, yet the New Forest stock somehow assimilated them all and remains today a recognized breed, tough and sturdy, short-necked and wide-shouldered with fine mane and tail.

Today they are left to mate with their own stallions. Beside the Agisters who look after their practical welfare, the New Forest Pony Breeding and Cattle Society promotes shows and point-to-point races and generally encourages the breeding of fine stock.

Since deer are so elusive, especially by day, the picture of the forest most often taken away by visitors will be a little group of ponies peacefully grazing a clearing by a wood's edge, whisking tails to keep the flies away or pushing through tall bracken, whickering to their foals to follow.

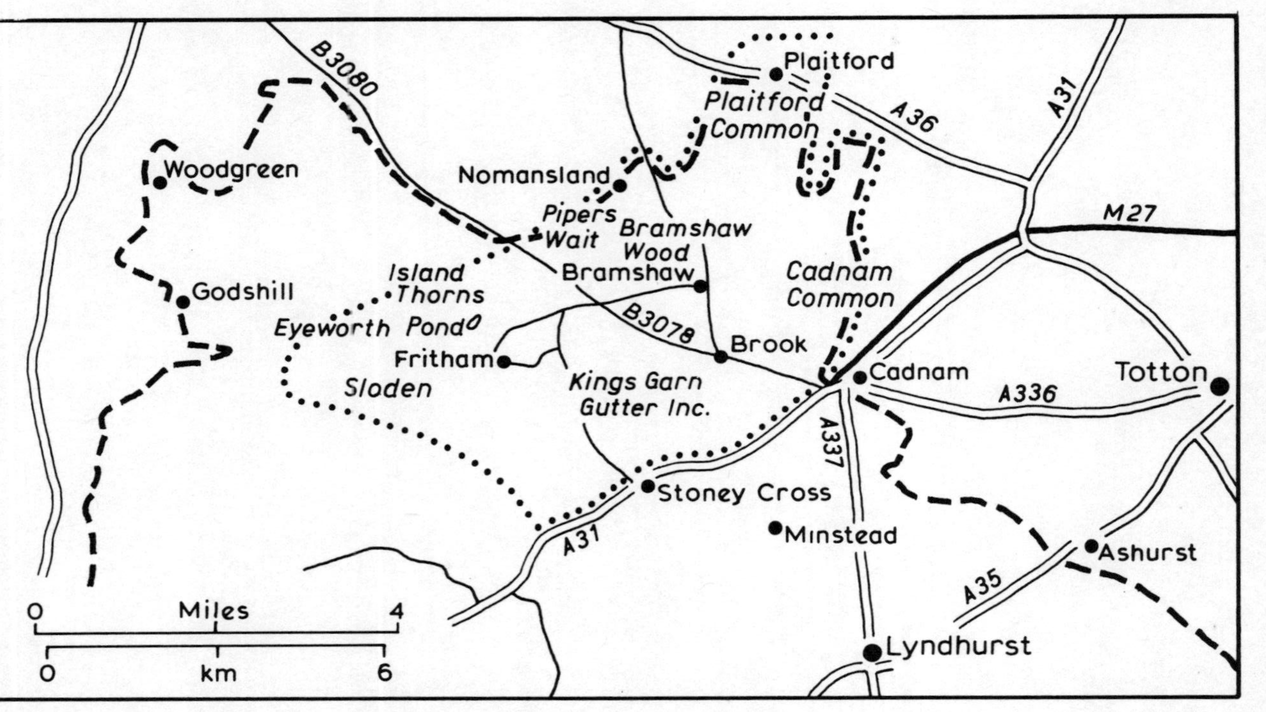

Bramshaw, Fritham and the North

8 *Bramshaw, Fritham and the North*

The leaves are falling in Amberwood and Sloden, Island Thorns and Ocknell: the visitors go home, leaving even Canterton Glen, that most visited spot, empty at last. You would expect the murder of a king to have taken place in some atmospheric glade among great oaks – somewhere like Mark Ash perhaps or among the majestic beeches of Woodfidley – so Canterton Glen comes as something of a shock.

The Rufus Stone stands on a patch of lawn fringed with scrub, close to the road and opposite a car-park, for once not hidden away. The monument itself is peculiarly ugly, the stone encased in iron to discourage vandals. It reads, 'Here stood the oak tree on which an arrow shot by Sir Walter Tyrrell at a stag glanced and struck King William II surnamed Rufus on the breast, of which he instantly died on August 2nd 1100.

'William II being slain was laid on a cart belonging to one Purkiss and drawn from hence to Winchester and buried in the Cathedral church of that city.'

Whatever the setting, the story as told by the old chroniclers is romantic enough. William, carousing at Malwood, dreams of blood: two monks also dreamt of disaster to the King. The Abbot of Shrewsbury even preached that, 'The bow of God's vengeance is bent against the wicked. The arrow, swift to wound, is already drawn out of the quiver.' Nevertheless, William went hunting and was killed by an arrow – only that is really certain.

Leland in his history maintains that the accident (murder, or ritual sacrifice, depending on your point of view) happened near Througham. For many years this was thought to be an old name for Fritham, which led to the Rufus Stone being erected in Canterton Glen, near that village.

However, recent research has upset all the old stories, Arthur Lloyd, a distinguished writer on the New Forest, and others have discovered that Througham was not Fritham at all but the old name for an area near Beaulieu Abbey now occupied by Park Farm – a document of 1606 mentions 'Beauley Park alias Througham'. This is supported by the fact that William is said to have been killed near a chapel. No such ruins have ever been found at Canterton, but Richard Warner, once the Rev. Gilpin's curate at Boldre, wrote in his *Topographic Remarks*, 1793, 'The chapel of Park Grange remains to this day, though in a dilapidated state.' No chapel remains have ever been traced to Canterton Glen.

Furthermore, Mr Lloyd has found an ancient Latin document which states, 'In the year 1204 King John once built a Cistercian Abbey which he named Bellus Locus, near the spot where William Rufus the King was killed.' Park Farm is only three miles from Bellus Locus, Beaulieu, whereas Canterton is more than ten.

So should the Rufus Stone be moved? The Park Farm area, a mile south of St Leonard's Grange, very near the coast, lies among flat marshlands and fields, even less characteristic of the real New Forest, though still within the bounds. Could this quiet agricultural area cope with the influx of visitors the stone would bring – for it is one of the most visited sites in the whole forest, a real honeypot.

Doubtless the pub at Canterton would prefer the stone to stay put: this handsome, half-timbered but modern inn is called after Sir Walter Tyrrell, who may or may not have shot the fatal arrow, which was meant to kill a red stag – or a red king. The death of William Rufus, where and why and how, will continue to fascinate historian and visitor alike, because so little hard fact is known and folklore takes over.

How do you alter folklore? Should someone tell Ocknell Pond not to turn blood red every August, it was all a mistake! And what of the terrible hound, able to pass straight through walls, the ghost of Walter Tyrrell's hound, which haunts the fabled glen?

Moving westward from stamped-over Canterton, we came to the heights of Stoney Cross, a wide, heathy plain with splendid views all round, high only by forest standards, with a real 'on top of the world' feel to it at only 370 feet. J.R. Wise in his source book *The New Forest*, waxes lyrical here: 'If anyone wishes to see the beauty of the Forest in autumn, let him see the view from the high ridge at Stoney Cross ... the maples are dyed yellow and russet by the autumn rains and the beeches are scorched to a fiery red with the first frost and the oaks renew the golden lights of spring, till the great woods of Prior's Acre and Daneshill burn with colour.'

Alongside the road lie extra stretches of tarmac, betraying the fact that this was yet one more wartime airfield. Built in 1942, it became a fighter station with Mustangs zooming into the sky where now only larks take off and bees bumble among the gorse blooms. In 1943 a squadron from Northern Rhodesia moved in, flying the famous Hurricanes. Later an airborne division of the army camped closed by, using the airfield to practise parachute drops and glider-towing. In 1941 American squadrons arrived, first fighters then bombers. After the war, taken over by Transport Command, it was busy with Wellingtons, Stirlings and Liberators, ferrying troops out to India and back home. It was closed down by the end of 1947, some of its runways adapted as minor roads which drive straight as an arrow across the heath.

Other stretches of hard standing have been taken over as camp sites. At Long Beech, caravans are spread out among oak, beech and holly, under an enormous water tank high on a tower, another legacy of the airfield. Further concrete makes a pleasant car-park by the small round pond called Janesmoor where in summer you can picnic at the tables provided on the grassy banks and admire the waterlilies.

Stoney Cross is vast and spacious, much grazed by ponies and cattle. One winter day we saw thirty fallow deer feeding on Ocknell Plain, till, startled by kite-flying children, they suddenly took off, streaming away in line astern like a living frieze. Lapwing fly in, instead of Hurricanes, and crows peck about a square of heathland which once held a cinema!

Besides Janesmoor, there is Ocknell Pond and enchanting Cadman's Pool, named after former Deputy Surveyor Arthur Cadman, author of *Dawn, Dusk and Deer*. The pool, sheltered by the beeches and hollies of Anses Wood to the north, open to the sun on the south, its banks curved in and out, green and random, is often home to Canada geese and the occasional kingfisher. You would not easily guess that this is yet one more man-made pond, dug to provide gravel for improvements to the nearby A31.

Out in the middle are two small islands covered with bracken, birch and small Scots pines. On our November visit these had been taken over by a large flock of chaffinches, the trees and banks all a-flicker with hundreds of wings as they feasted on the beech mast. Fieldfare had flown in too, those silvery winter visitors, and a few black-headed gulls which visit whatever the season. Paths wander off to Anses Wood and down to Holly Hatch Inclosure. Since cars can park right by the water, Cadman's Pool is a fine picnic place, winter or summer.

Though Scots pine grew in southern Britain in prehistoric times, it afterwards seems to have died out. When Ocknell Wood was planted in 1775, a few Scots pine were introduced to see if they would grow in the forest! Anyone who has walked through the dark and sterile-floored monotony of Forestry Commission plantations will give a bitter laugh. But the Ocknell Clump has a certain dignity; in fact, if you can bring yourself to look at a Scots pine growing in isolation, it does appear a tree of character with its orange bark, adding an oriental touch to the landscape, a hint of Japanese plate design – it is only in uniform rows the trees shed such gloom.

More of the old airfield hard standing has been utilized, on the fringe of Ocknell Wood, for Ocknell camp site, but turning east we set out to walk to the hamlet of Brook without touching tarmac, old or new. Our path led down a driftway between Coppice of Linwood and Kings Garn Gutter Inclosures, with a vast view to the north-east towards Romsey and the far side of the River Test valley, gradually receding as we moved downhill. The driftway is more than a hundred yards wide between mixed woodland, dark pines against yellow sycamore, the ground humped with molehills, patched with fading bracken and bramble, a kestrel hovering overhead.

Down in the valley bottom, where even the November air feels mild, it is so sheltered, runs Kings Garn Gutter, a little stream well known as rich hunting ground for fossil-hunters. 'Garn' is said to be an abbreviated form of 'garden', so perhaps this was the king's bee garden, one of the places in the forest where the hives were set out in spring.

In summer we often come to a wood nearby – to listen, for this is the home of the New Forest cicada, an insect discovered in 1812, when it lived in sheltered woods around Brockenhurst, seldom seen but betraying its presence by a peculiar high-pitched whirring 'song'. In 1940 this summer sound was not heard, though, and for twenty-two years the cicada was unknown and thought to be extinct in Britain, till in 1962 it reappeared in these woods, where it is now protected and studied. Its curious life history begins with a pale crest of egg-nests along a hanging beech or birch twig. As soon as the eggs hatch, the tiny grubs or 'nymphs' drop to the ground and dig their way into the soil, where they find juicy roots of molinia grass to suck. There they remain for several years, possibly seven or more, until they are already to climb up into the light, shed their old skin and become flying, singing cicadas.

Wandering on, we come to Gibbet Wood, which presently thins away, and we are suddenly out in the open, in fact on the mown turf of Bramshaw Golf Course. There really was a gibbet: it stood here by the fourteenth tee. Some say the last man to be hanged on it was a horse-thief, others a murderer who had robbed an old woman, then set fire to her house.

Crossing the golf course we come to the hamlet of Brook. A white-railed bridge spans the brook, overhung with trees, a thatched cottage on either bank, with the eighteenth-century Green Dragon opposite, thatched and whitewashed with big green shutters. The little stream, having collected the waters of Kings Garn Gutter and Coalmeer Gutter, eventually becomes the Cadnam River which we had crossed in Conan Doyle's old garden. Apart from this pretty bridge corner, Brook is a scatter of cottages, bungalows, farms and the Bell, a Georgian-style hotel, catering particularly for golfers.

Thirsty after our walk from Ocknell, we visited the Green Dragon, a cosy, inviting pub with red carpet, a log fire in a vast stone fireplace and hot snacks on offer. Low beams, small bars and copper tankards add to ye olde atmosphere. On the walls hang facsimiles of historic forest documents, such as the petition against winter heyning, 1852 – a law demanding the removal of all livestock from the forest during the winter months, though seldom enforced. Above all, it is a horsy pub. The walls are hung with leather panels stamped with commoners' brand marks which identify ponies running on the forest to their owners and to the Agisters. There is also a fine display of rosettes, so it is no surprise to learn that this is the regular meeting place for the New Forest Pony Breeding and Cattle Society. 'Green Dragon', like the more common 'Red Lion', is a name derived from heraldry, in this case part of the arms of the Earls of Pembroke whose seat is at Wilton House near Salisbury.

Branching right, the road climbs uphill to Bramshaw, between fields and farms now, so it is obvious we are on the very edge of the forest. There are cottages, new bungalows, a garage, the village hall strung at intervals on either side. Two lodges mark entrances to Fountains Court, a beautiful farmhouse in landscaped grounds built in 1918. The other treasures must be sought out.

In the Domesday survey, Ulnod held land in Bramshaw worth ten shillings. The first family to leave its mark were the Warrens, who held property from the sixteenth century and gave their name to the house later bought by Mr George Eyre, a name famous ever since in these parts. The Eyres built their own mansion, designed by Nash, on the Warrens' site. To reach this you have to turn off the main road and find Stocks Cross. Here stood the village stocks, and also another gallows, though we are still close to Gibbet Hill! Was this once a place rife with crime? Turning off here, we come into parkland, drives leading off between close-clipped rhododendron hedges, and the house comes into view, elegant primrose brick with tall, rounded windows. An archway leads into a square stableyard complete with clock, now estate offices.

Living in the New Forest

Hyde Silver Band, Moyles Court

Market Day at Ringwood

British Driving Society at Park Hill

(*Opposite*) New Forest Show, New Park: Woodmans' Competition

New Forest Show, New Park: Light Trade Turnouts

Until recently the Roman Catholic chapel here was open to the local people – a footpath leads straight across to the village, but this has recently been pulled down. The house was for many years the home of Sir Oliver Crosthwaite Eyre, chairman of the publishers Eyre & Spottiswoode but better known locally as a Verderer and a Member of Parliament for the New Forest till 1968, after which he emigrated to Rhodesia, but the family still occupy Warrens.

Many visitors must pass through Bramshaw and conclude that it does not have a church, but it is worth the long climb out beyond the village to find – it may not be an architectural gem but it is full of interest. To begin with, it stands on a commanding position on a natural bluff which seems the higher because the road has carved a deep channel beneath. From the churchyard gentle green farmland falls away to the north, but to the south Bramshaw Wood covers all the hill beyond, yellow and brown and russet in its autumn colours.

Tradition maintains there was a church here even before the Normans came and that William Rufus, the most hated of monarchs, stabled his horses in it. The earliest real mention is in 1158, when the church's ownership was transferred from a suppressed priory to Salisbury Cathedral, the Dean and Chapter being thus able to claim forest privileges. In 1649 they were bound 'to provide a sufficient curate and minister of honest and good reputation who was to be paid eight pounds a year and be provided with house and gardens. He was entitled to tithe eggs, all fees and Easter offerings.'

The church is cruciform, the oldest stone and flint walls reinforced with later brick. A great reconstruction in 1829 demolished the south transept and belfry, rebuilding it in brick. In the small tiled entrance is a drawing of the old church made in 1805 which shows a little pointed wooden spire on a hipped roof. Inside, the roof is unexpectedly low, because of a gallery above – this is the south transept. Another gallery hangs above the west end. The north transept was built by the Eyres of Warrens: hatchments and memorial tablets cover the walls. In 1912 seven young men from Bramshaw decided to emigrate to the New World: there is a monument to them all, drowned on

Brockenhurst Church

the *Titanic*. A wooden staircase leads up to the bellringers' loft – only two bells but the treble dates from 1250 and still rings true.

Further up the hill a narrow road turns off to the left and winds up through the woods, the ancient oaks and beeches of Bramshaw, some of which provided the roof timbers for Salisbury Cathedral in the early thirteenth century. The woodland floor is bright with fallen beech leaves, except where the pigs have been rootling or where holly forms a dark understorey.

We emerge in Nomansland, said to have been left out of any keeper's charge because it is on the forest edge and so gained its name. It is unusual also in shape. All the buildings, red brick cottages, a Methodist chapel, bungalows, 'The Lamb' with thatched porches, real ale and a garden, stand on the north-west side of the road, facing a wide green with a cricket pitch in the middle, which stretches across to the edge of Bramshaw Wood.

Nomansland is high, bracing and windy, not far from the forest's highest point at Piper's Wait. A vast view stretches away north-eastwards into blue distances only slightly marred by a line of pylons marching across the common beyond. One of the houses here is called Boundary Cottage – in fact the boundary of the forest is the road line. We go down it towards the commons, land which used not to be included within the perambulation.

All along this northern edge are stretches of heathland, some four thousand acres which were originally outside the boundary of the New Forest, and known as the Commons Adjacent. Here those with commoners' rights could pasture cattle and ponies free: if their stock wandered into the New Forest, they were also getting free grazing at the expense of the forest commoners who had to pay a fee for each animal when it was tail-marked by the Agisters. This led to constant friction, especially after the last war, when the New Forest commoners set out to have all their animals tuberculosis tested. In fact it was not until 1956 that the whole forest could claim to be a TT area, partly because of difficulties with infected cattle wandering in off the commons.

Briscoe Eyre, of Warrens, had given some of the common lands round Bramshaw to the National Trust, who already owned several hundred acres nearby.

We had already visited Cadnam Common from the pony round-up and made this time for Plaitford (pronounced Playford), the largest of the commons, for this is now inside the forest perambulation.

In 1964 Sir Oliver Crosthwaite Eyre was largely responsible for getting the New Forest Act through Parliament. Under this, the northern commoners agreed that their lands should be included within the New Forest in return for concessions on marking fees and a promise that the entire new boundary would be furnished with cattlegrids which would solve the problem of straying. The Bill was bitterly fought by those commoners who felt they were losing their hereditary rights, and though all this is old history now, there are still deep feelings in these parts. We were told, in lowered voices, of attempts to mark a boundary with broken glass, of fences uprooted at dead of night.

Plaitford is one of those villages, like Exbury, which has moved: we had to seek half a mile down narrow lanes for their original settlement, for today the village is mostly strung along the main Southampton to Salisbury Road. It was once called Playdeford, the manor held for the service of keeping Melchet Park, to the north. As there was no church at Melchet, the estate workers and family attended Plaitford church, where they had a special pew but declined to pay tithes so that commissioners were sent by the Crown in 1619 to enforce the payment of twenty shillings every Easter.

The manor at one time belonged to the Compton family of Minstead: it was sold to Sir Stephen Fox, Charles II's Paymaster. Today old Plaitford is a handsome brick farmhouse – Manor Farm, with a thatched barn still perched on staddle stones, near the River Blackwater, and the church, parts of which date from the thirteenth century. It is built mostly of flint, topped by a tiny wooden spire and flanked by an immense, ancient yew tree, its branches almost sweeping the grass. Inside there is a raked gallery at the west end; beneath it an area has been stripped of pews and curtained off, and here still stands an original window. The rest has been much restored, though still plain and pleasing with whitewashed walls and clear-leaded windows which look out on tall cypress with fields beyond.

Most of present-day Plaitford is modern, with a pub called 'The Shoe', bungalows, nurseries, farms and breeding kennels, but on the south side a narrow stretch of heath is named Plaitford Common with a National Trust sign. This is much more interesting than it appears, for soon the boundary drops away and the walker is rewarded with a wide expanse of heather and gorse, grassland and bog.

Today it is wrapped in still November fog, only a robin singing from a young birch. A sandy boundary bank is deep holed by rabbit and badger: old gorse stems sprout the yellow jelly blobs called Witches Butter, and on a birch we find bracket fungus, called Razor Strop. Ponies have cropped the grass short as a lawn but out in the middle grass gives way to bog; runnels and little pools lie everywhere, some of them permanent enough to grow flote grass – like most of the forest most of the time, Plaitford Common can only be explored comfortably in boots.

Far to the south a dark shape looming through the fog is the rise of Bramshaw Wood, while near at hand the bare stems of bog myrtle glow a deep wine colour through the grey air, and a kestrel hovers over tussocks of molinia grass intent on flick of small tail or whisker. On the way back we pass a stand of turkey oaks, green-stained bark fissured into diamond patterns, the cracks a bright tangerine and the ground beneath littered with brown leaves more deeply lobed than the common oak.

Though we do not glimpse any deer today, they were here not long ago, stripping bark from a holly tree – the wound is still fresh: strange to think this whole stretch of country could not have been included within the forest before 1964.

Circling the commons has brought us back to Bramshaw Wood and the hill above it, Piper's Wait, a heathery plateau which at 422 feet is the highest point in the New Forest. Up here, wandering between the pits of old gravel workings and patches of birch or pine scrub to find the best vantage points, we looked out over a great sea of woodland fading to winter's brown now but still here and there patched with yellow, or the dark of pines. Northward lie the hills of Wiltshire, southward the distant island downs.

Telegraph Hill, to the west, only a few feet lower, was the site of a semaphore station early in the nineteenth century. This was one in a chain of signal masts joining London to Plymouth. The line from Bramshaw Telegraph north-eastward joined up with the Portsmouth to London line beyond Monkwood Binstead. By a code of some sixty-seven signals, Greenwich time could be flashed to Portsmouth in forty-five seconds – when the electric telegraph was introduced, Members of Parliament were worried that it might not be as speedy as the old system, which in its turn had superseded the beacon bonfires of Elizabethan times.

From the summit we set out to walk to Fritham, down across undulating heathland into Studley Wood. From the knotted old Scots pines along the edge, wood pigeons flap into the air, always the first to warn of intruders. Here and there among the oaks a yew still holds bright pink berries. Climbing away from the path, we paid a visit to Studley Castle – there is no entrance fee! Indeed, anyone used to the splendours of Carisbrooke or Caernarvon will scarcely recognize it. A low mossy bank, broken in places, bounds a small raised area holding – more trees. For a long time this little enclosure, like similar ones in Sloden and Roe Wood, was held to be the remains of an ancient cattle pound. Studley is now reckoned to be the site of a royal hunting lodge in medieval times. Probably this grand name is as misleading as castle, and signifies nothing more than a thatched wooden hut where a hunting party could camp for the night.

We made a detour to the west, leaving the wood temporarily to find The Butts. All along the edge where tree met heath, the leaves lay in lacy frost patterns, every vein picked out with white, shining threads, bracken the most intricate, then oak. The heath shone with a thousand puddles – their thin ice crackled beneath our boots. The Butts are a group of prehistorical burial mounds, but they have eroded away over the centuries, excavation has removed their summits and they are altogether easy to miss in the rolling landscape, but one has a small thorn tree growing on the top.

Back in the woods we turn eastward through Eyeworth, full of ancient oaks, and beeches, the beech husks crunching underfoot.

Leaves drop from the air, yellow, brown, scarlet, and a squirrel freezes at sight of us, tail high, before whisking off up an oak towards an untidy-looking drey in its fork. Another oak had housed a lesser spotted woodpecker's nest – the previous June their young ones had taken turns to pop their heads out of the hole while the parents hopped about anxiously below, trying to persuade them to fly down, but there were no woodpeckers today, only a flock of redwing jinking over, a wren scolding from the hollies and a nuthatch tap-tapping away high overhead.

Some of the trees are three hundred years old, their roots mantled in moss: here a giant has fallen, letting in the sun. Though the frost will kill most of the fungi, there are still little pearls of beech tuft on the dead tree, and white candlesnuff amongst the invading moss and ferns.

A flourishing understorey of holly darkens the wood ahead, bright with berries though, a bumper crop this year. Soon dealers will tender with the Forestry Commission for the right to cut holly in a particular area, overseen by a keeper, and some of the forest berries will be hacked down, piled into trucks and sold in the towns. Likewise infant Norway spruce will be cut for Christmas trees – a quick cash crop – from the Rhinefield plantations and others. Sometimes a special order comes in for a municipal tree, and one must be found of an exact height, but most are sent over to Ringwood Forest where they are sold direct to the public, as many as three thousand a season. Lately there has been less demand for local trees because of heavy imports of high-quality trees from Europe. Sent over by the container load, these are often cheaper than our own Forestry Commission trees.

One more job for the keepers as Christmas approaches is to organize patrols round plantations to discourage wholesale theft of Norway spruce, for a lorry load of these is a valuable commodity.

As we came toward the edge of Eyeworth, two roe deer bound away, in their dark buff-brown winter coats: we disturbed their fruit-picking, for a few bright crab apples still hang on a tree here, by a stand of white beam. Some of the older inhabitants of Fritham still call this nearby wood by its old name, which sounds like Iver, in Domesday Book Ivare. In the reign of Henry III, one Roger Beteston held land then spelled Yvez, by virtue of finding litter for the King's bed and hay for his horse when he came to this part of the forest to hunt.

Fritham hamlet straggles up hill and down, its most striking building being Fritham House, white walled with tall chimneys, all that can be glimpsed behind imposing estate walls of red brick which form an arched entrance and nearby include a picturesque tower – which actually houses a water tank! Fritham House was for many years the house of Sir Timothy Eden, brother to Sir Antony. It looks out on a green scattered with ancient oaks and a meeting of lanes.

One of these winds between farms and cottages, then climbs up to the Royal Oak, a small thatched pub with a long, narrow bar and wooden benches along the walls, part of which is really old, the walls of traditional mud and wattle. The fireplace has a hearth four feet wide to accommodate four-foot lengths of cord wood, since the pub can claim forest rights. It used to burn a cartload of faggots a week. It can also claim rights of mast – that is, turning out pigs in the autumn, rights of pasture and rights of turbary, or cutting turf; in fact, this was one of the few houses we found which had within recent years exercised this right and actually burned turf or peat – all of which sorted oddly with Marley tiles and a juke box!

Here in the north of the forest, almost surrounded by great stretches of woodland, one does not immediately think of smuggling, but as a crow flies we are only some twelve miles inland. One of the most bloodthirsty tales of the eighteenth century involves the Royal Oak.

A smuggler's ship complete with cargo was caught in the English Channel and towed into Poole Harbour, where the captured brandy, tea and lace were impounded in the Customs House and the men thrown into jail to await their trial. But the smugglers had many friends in the forest. As soon as they heard the news, they banded together, armed themselves and set off on horseback to collect reinforcements. They left Lyndhurst and rode through Minstead to Fritham, where they drank early at the Royal Oak, then slipped down through Amberwood and

Sloden, thence in darkness to Poole.

Overpowering the guards at the Customs House, they recovered their brandy, tea and lace, loading up the horses, after which they attacked the jail, rescued the smugglers and made off up the Avon valley in high spirits, stopping at the George Inn, Fordingbridge, to divide the booty and celebrate their victory. But they celebrated too long – soldiers and Customs officers caught up with them and a pitched battle took place in Bridge Street, some of the smugglers being killed.

However, the ringleaders escaped with much of the smuggled goods, which they hastily dropped off with friends in the forest. The authorities, angry at this double defeat, offered a reward and free pardon for information. A few 'turned their coats', revealing that the leaders had taken refuge in Frogham, but news, somehow, by secret forest ways, travelled faster than excise men. Fore warned, the smugglers ambushed them on the ridge by Bramshaw, and they rounded up the turncoats, beat them to death and buried them in an old gravel pit.

A few returned to Fritham.

For in the end this is a moral tale: the gang was eventually captured. Then, to spread the news as widely as possible that crime does not pay, the smugglers were hanged in chains, at Godshill, Breamore, Poole – and Fritham.

Above the Royal Oak, three tracks fan out across the wide green where a litter of minute piglets are making the most of their rights of pannage among strutting bantams and one mild-mannered goose. This is a lovely, peaceful scene; the tracks wander off into the forest so there is little traffic; there are wooden seats ranged round ready for a picnic or an idle moment; encircling woods shelter from the wind.

We take the right-hand track, which is tarmac but only for a short way. This plunges downhill to Eyeworth Pond. A car-park fronts the water, and on an inviting hummocky hillock behind, one of those discreet dark green Forestry Commission notices says 'Picnic Area', as if you might not have recognized it.

Eyeworth Pond is perhaps our favourite forest water. On the far bank oaks and alders grow right down to the lake's edge; out in the middle are several tiny islands, willow-hung and reedy, while the far end merges into shallows and marsh with stands of great reed mace – all of which makes splendid cover for birds. The ducks are half tame from being fed the leftovers of countless picnics. Today there are mallard, brown pintails with the unmistakable long tail feathers, compact little wigeon with chestnut heads, and dark-backed tufted ducks with the swept-back hairstyle. Moorhens skulk about the reeds, and coot disappear with loud kyowks but the ducks swim toward us, beady eyes hopeful – picnickers are scarce in November.

Locals often refer to the whole pond as Irons Well. This is really the name of the spring which helps provide water for the pond. Long before there was a pond, the spring was renowned for its medicinal, even magical qualities and used to treat sore eyes, rheumatism and skin disease. It is even suggested there was once a lepers' hospital here, where the victims could be treated by the water, but no remains have ever been found.

We walked along the track which passes the spring. It is not so easy to find now since it has been neglected and a tree fallen partly across: many small ditches and streamlets actually feed the pond, but once glimpsed, the spring is unmistakable, bubbling up just below the path a fierce orange colour, stained with iron – no wonder it was thought to cure even leprosy.

The track, which is firm walking even in winter, leads out to Howen Bottom, a marshy valley below the ridge of Piper's Wait patched with small woods called hats in forest terms. Great castles of white cumulus are piled round the horizon, making the ridge seem higher: a flight of redwing jink over against a cold blue sky, and out on the heath a silvery hen-harrier, wings dark tipped, sails low over the winter brown heather and suddenly drops, on vole or meadow pippit, we cannot tell.

Retracing our steps, we soon glimpse the shining level of Eyeworth, hear splashings, quack, the shy prrp of moorhen. You cannot but rejoice that men made this pond, but who, with a thousand chances, would ever guess why it came into being more than a hundred years ago? The clues are there, for those who can read them – a few wooden huts on the other side of the road.

From the road it is possible to see how the pond has been made by raising a large bank to dam back the waters of Irons Well and various small streams. Water lips over a spillway and runs down concrete steps to a leat beneath the road. This was all constructed to supply water power to – a gunpowder factory.

Powder Mills, on Dartmoor, were built with massive stone walls to contain any explosion, since granite lay all about; only the roofs were deliberately flimsy. Here in the forest the builders also used what was to hand: the whole works consisted of a series of wooden huts, well dispersed so that, in case of accident, one would not ignite another – the magazine or store was the only exception, brick-lined inside a mound of earth.

The works were founded by a German, Captain Schultz, and at first made gunpowder for the German army, involved in 1870 in the Franco-Prussian war. Afterwards it specialized in smokeless powder for sporting guns, until 1914 when it was taken over by the British Government.

Water power helped grind the constituents, sulphur, saltpetre and charcoal, of which there were ready supplies to hand. During the war gunpowder was supplied to the troops in Flanders, and work was at its height. A hundred and forty men were employed in day and night shifts, walking in from Hyde, Cadnam and miles around, for, because the work was dangerous and there were casualties from time to time, they were paid five shillings a week more than the average manual worker's wage. A gatekeeper searched each worker for matches as he came in. The working clothes were leather boots without studs and black overalls. The zinc-lined containers weighed one hundredweight empty: a wagon load of them full was too heavy to be pulled up the steep rise into Fritham village, so a new track was made alongside the pond, by which the wagons reached Redlynch station. One of the larger buildings was the stables, housing up to fifty horses used in transporting the powder.

Some of the cottages in Fritham and the chapel were built specially for the factory workers, in 1904. Old photographs of the works show a complex of long, low buildings and wooden huts grouped near the manager's house, an attractive building gabled and turreted – and there it is still, now called Eyeworth Lodge. An increasing use of dynamite and the end of the war brought far less demand for gunpowder, and the works were eventually moved to Scotland, most of the huts being demolished – a few remain in the fields used variously for hens or horses.

Joan Begbie, writing in 1934, blamed the decline of salmon in a western forest stream on Captain Schultz: 'Once the proud salmon came to spawn, finding the gravelly depths perfect for nurseries. The powder mills built near Fritham a long while ago so tainted the water that cattle refused to drink it, and the fish holding their noses, fled, never, in the case of the salmon, to return.' But then we are indebted to the captain for beautiful Eyeworth Pond.

West of Fritham lie great woods, Island Thorns and Ashley Rails, Sloden and Amberwood. All round like hummocks and banks, signs of the large Romano-British pottery kilns which were built here in the third and fourth centuries, their bowls and bottles, storage jars and dishes being in demand all over southern Britain. Some of the pottery was of a much finer quality than the coarse vessels produced at Rough Piece which we saw earlier. Some of the Island Thorns pottery was elegant in shape, evidently turned on a wheel and ornamented with a rich variety of patterns, chains and scrolls, interlacing circles and fern leaves.

In the Red House Museum at Christchurch there are coarse pots from Sloden and in contrast the more refined products of the kilns at Ashley Rails, a pale buff and smooth to touch, some bearing a delicate daisy pattern or lattice work, others ornamented with clay slip.

When we walked down into Amberwood, we moved stealthily, often freezing against the bole of some tall beech, not evading Roman ghosts but stalking deer, with a camera. Fallow are the commonest deer in the forest, yet they are so elusive by daylight it is always a delight to glimpse even one. October and November are good months for deer-watching, since this is when the buck can be found with his harem of females and the rut or mating begins.

On a still, misty day the wood was truly amber, bracken fading to pale browns, oak and beech leaves, yellow and tawny, dropping slowly through the damp air, patterning the forest floor with colour – except in one place where it was black – we had found a rutting scrape.

For hundreds, even thousands of years, fallow deer have moved through our woods, silent as shadows. Their fossil bones have been found in Ice Age deposits in Britain though not in strata laid down later. Possibly the natives were wiped out by the cold and Britain was re-populated from Europe while there was still a land bridge, or perhaps, as many books suggest, they were brought over by the Romans. By the time this land was proclaimed a New Forest, fallow roamed wild. Later they became a status symbol of the time, many manor houses running their own herds in parkland. The ill wind of war often brought freedom to these confined herds; taking advantage of neglected fences or walls destroyed by Cromwell's army, they galloped off to augment the native stock, so that in the New Forest alone our keeper friend had estimated some nine hundred at the spring census.

Even so, thousands of visitors to the forest leave again without sight of a single deer. The sanctuary at Bolderwood is your best chance, otherwise remember they move out of cover at twilight. Like birds, fallow do not worry much about a stationary car and will trot unconcernedly past, so it makes a good hide. Most of the year they are very quiet animals, a doe gently whickering to its fawn perhaps: the most startling sound made by a doe is its bark, so deep and sudden it resembles a shot going off. This means she is anxious, or suspicious – an eerie sound at dusk.

Only once a year does the buck become vocal: this is in October when the mating season begins; then he starts 'groaning', a strange guttral moaning sound almost like belching which we had heard night after night in the woods during the last few weeks – on a still night it will carry half a mile or more. At this time the buck returns to his rutting place, or stand, of the previous year. This one in Amberwood is some sixty feet across under a grove of Scots pine, the ground churned into a morass of black, trampled mud, the trunks flayed where bucks had threshed with their antlers, marking out their rutting territory and leaving the scent from glands below the eye.

Fallow are fascinating to watch because there is still a great deal to be learned about their behaviour: what we actually observed would often contradict accounts in books, and today was no exception. Though it was getting late in the season for rutting, an air of excitement swept through the great wood, little bands of does stealing across rides, a buck groaning some way off as the low clouds turned a dull orange in the west.

Presently two bucks appeared side by side moving along a ride a quarter of a mile from the rutting stand. One was a fine specimen with tall antlers, probably a 'great buck' in deer parlance, meaning five years old or more, the other slighter and younger. They trotted purposefully toward the centre of excitement but at a meeting of rides turned off into the trees, faced each other and began to fight with much crashing of antlers and sounds of heavy breathing. We expected the older buck to emerge triumphant and quickly make for the rutting stand while the younger ran off. However, after more groaning and clashing the two bucks appeared, side by side, and ran off, back the way they had come!

Five does crossed the ride, moving hopefully the other way. The fawns will be born, usually singly, from the end of May, the doe going off by herself. The fawn will spend its early days lying still in deep cover – its only hope of surviving this most vulnerable time, utterly defenceless against dog or fox. By this time the bucks will have cast their antlers, sometimes gnawing at them, not to waste the precious calcium needed to grow the next set. Towards the end of August these will have finished growing, then the bucks thresh them about to rub off the covering velvet, damaging the smaller trees. They also strip off bark to eat when other food is scarce, in winter.

Later in the year, Amberwood lay brown and still, a last leaf falling here and there and Latchmore Brook trickling ale-coloured between bare banks. After all the excitement of the rut, the bucks will have gone off alone to recuperate before gathering together in male herds. The does and their half-grown fawns will be elsewhere in their herds.

Under the interwoven canopy of Amberwood, we had scarcely noticed the snow powdering down, but turning along Latchmore Bottom we came into the pines of Alderhill Inclosure, and here the world was transformed, each ride a white pathway, each horizontal branch sprinkled with white like a Christmas decoration. Alderhill is not a regimented plantation, ploughed and sown in straight lines. When the original oak was felled, some Scots pine and a few Douglas fir were left to reproduce naturally, and this they did so well that trees are in some places only inches apart. 'Thick as mustard and cress,' an ex-forester was heard to remark. You can recognize the mature, mother trees here and there, outtopping the rest, while along the ridges grow dense little pyramidal bushes – of pine needles. These are seedling pines repeatedly topped by browsing deer, so that, unable to grow upwards, they have thickened out at the base.

All is still, not so much as a robin stirring until we cross the brook when a wisp of snipe whirr up almost from beneath our feet and wing away affronted, crying, 'Scaap-scaap!'

Branching left, we come out of the trees onto open heathland, the steep flank of Hampton Ridge, the snowy landscape broken up by dark patches of old heather, gorse thickets and one completely circular pond, with a willow growing up through the centre of it – nature repairing the ravages of war – for this was a bomb crater. Soon after the beginning of the last war, five thousand acres of forest up here were taken over as a practice bombing range: later even more land was acquired. Further along Hampton Ridge the concrete target mound can still be seen among the furze.

A steep climb brings us up into a good track running the length of the ridge, frozen puddles cracking under our boots as they cracked long ago under Roman sandals, for this is an ancient road, old even when it was the highway for pottery from Island Thorns and Ashley Rails on its road to the Avon valley and beyond.

Hampton is only some three hundred feet high, yet we look out over vast stretches of heath and woodland, ridge and valley. Some of those far gorsy slopes are home to the rare Dartford warbler, a dark little bird with rufous breast seen only in the south of England and the only warbler to stay with us all year, though today there will be few insects about for him to eat. Kestrel, buzzard and hobby hunt over the ridge: once, in early spring, we saw four buzzards overhead, lazily circling round together on their blunt wings and mewing to each other – a courting party.

Here are the familiar landmarks, the great sweep of Deadman's Hill to the north, the dark curve of Pitts Wood, the far hills of Dorset gleaming white, and southward, across the snowy slopes of Latchmore Bottom, the tattered pines of Hasley against the sky. Here in this wildest corner, in the first chill days of spring, we began to discover something of the New Forest: now we have come full circle with the turning year. Twilight gathers eastward over Amberwood and Sloden, a tawny owl calls from Alderhill and we turn for home, leaving the land to its secrets.

Further Reading

Walking in the New Forest, Joan Begbie (Maclehose & Co., 1934)

Wanderers in the New Forest, Juliette de Bairacli Levy (Faber & Faber, 1958)

The New Forest, A Symposium (Galley Press, 1960)

The New Forest – An Ecological History, Colin R. Tubbs (David & Charles, 1968)

Portrait of the New Forest, Brian Vesey-Fitzgerald (Robert Hale, 1969)

The New Forest, Its History and Scenery, John R. Wise (1883, republished by S.R. Publishers Ltd, 1971)

The New Forest, Heywood Sumner (1924, reprinted by Dolphin Press, 1972)

Verderers of the New Forest, Antony Pasmore (Pioneer Publications, 1977)

New Forest Documents, AD 1244-1334, ed. D.J. Stagg (Hampshire County Council, 1979)

Index